MINIATURE SCHNAUZERS
TODAY

Peter Newman

Howell Book House

HOWELL
BOOK
HOUSE

New York

HOWELL BOOK HOUSE
A Simon & Schuster / Macmillan Company
1633 Broadway
New York, NY 10019

MACMILLAN is a registered trademark of Macmillan, Inc.

Library of Congress Cataloging-in-Publication Data

Newman, Peter.
    Miniature schnauzers today / Peter Newman.
        p.   cm.
    ISBN 0–87605–239–1
    1. Miniature schnauzer. I. Title
SF429.M58N48 1997
636.755--dc21   97–34517
                                    CIP

Manufactured in Singapore

10 9 8 7 6 5 4 3 2 1

Contents

ACKNOWLEDGEMENTS

My most grateful thanks to the many dedicated Miniature breeders who have willingly helped, for, without their interest and support, this book would certainly not have been possible.

I would like to place on record my very special thanks to Dan Kiedrowski, who has been ever-helpful with information and photographs; his excellent breed classic *The New Miniature Schnauzer* (Howell Book House), an in-depth study of the breed in America, has been a most helpful reference source. My very special thanks also to Andrew Brace who has been fully supportive and helpful when most needed, as well as to Martin Butler for his splendid drawings and illustrations, especially to illustrate the Breed Standard, and also to Shaune Frost for all his help with the grooming and trimming photographs.

Ewa-Marie Knackholm, Pauline Bjoerklund and Angel Pons are also all deserving of special thanks for their support and helpfulness.

American-bred Ch. Irrenhaus Impact at Risepark (Am. Ch. Irrenhaus Stamp of Approval ex Am. Ch. Irrenhaus Bluet).
Bred by Mrs J. Hicks, owned by Mrs. Newman.
The only Miniature owned by the author's mother, finished in 1982 at 2 years of age (6 months of which were spent in quarantine). 'Hickey', a breed legend, won 7 Challenge Certificates, went Best in Show at the Schnauzer Club Specialty and sired eleven English Champions.

Photo: Sally Anne Thompson.

INTRODUCTION

The Miniature Schnauzer has a charm, and an endearing and captivating personality, that is all its own, which has ensnared its devotees and owners over the years and across the world. It is a sensible, thinking, highly intelligent and affectionate breed, but not over-demanding, and its splendid temperament, loyalty and adaptability have all been developed to a high degree.

The Miniature Schnauzer is certainly a quick learner, but does soon tire of repetition done for its own sake. These dogs adapt well to town or country living, live happily in numbers or as a single companion and make an excellent and delightful family dog.

Ch. Catalanta True Luck at Risepark. Bred by Mr & Mrs S. Saville, owned by Peter Newman.

Photo: Sally Anne Thompson.

Many of the qualities already recognised and highly valued in the Standard (or middle-sized) Schnauzer were handed down and retained in the Miniature when it was first being developed by the breed's Bavarian pioneers, in what is today Southern Germany, during the late nineteenth century.

These qualities were also recognised, and still further enhanced, by the early small band of American pioneer enthusiasts from the 1930s onwards, thus ensuring that the essential Schnauzer qualities and charm were recognised, well-ingrained and appreciated in the Miniature Schnauzer before the breed's popularity really took off.

Now some of these qualities and the dog's special charm, along with type and shape, have surely gone far enough down the road of change for those seriously concerned for the breed to reassess this trend.

A handy-sized breed with a sturdy body, the Miniature Schnauzer has the look of a terrier but is not similar in either structure or temperament. Its unique pepper and salt (shades of grey with silver furnishings), or the black and silver or solid black colouring, along with a harsh, easily workable coat, have all added to the attraction and appeal that the breed enjoys, while the grooming needed for smartness appeals to those who enjoy a degree of challenge and the satisfaction from a job well done.

Those seeking an excellent family dog, or a smart and stylish show dog, need look no further than the Miniature Schnauzer.

1 *BREED BEGINNINGS*

All breeds of pedigree dog are only pure-bred for so many generations. Indeed, if we had the ability to trace any breed right back to its origins, we would discover that all breeds do, in fact, eventually have common ancestors. The fact that we have, today, so many different breeds – almost one hundred and fifty recognised by the Kennel Club in Britain and the American Kennel Club, but about three times that number by the Fédération Cynologique Internationale – is due to generations of selective breeding. Some breeds became established as a consistent type through a rather haphazard, almost accidental, process. Others were rigidly selected for their working ability. Only the Toy breeds were chosen for their purely aesthetic qualities – but then they, too, had to be fit and hardy enough to perform certain fundamental tasks.

There are few breeds whose early development is carefully and accurately documented, so much of the "history" of any modern breed is subject to a degree of speculation and conjecture. The Miniature Schnauzer is no exception. One school of thought is that the Miniature was developed as a separate variety by breeding from only the smallest Schnauzer specimens – what is today known as the Standard, or Middle, size – until the breed had been bantamised and then it was bred consistently and true to the smaller size. Others have proffered the theory that the Schnauzer was crossed with smaller breeds, particularly the Affenpinscher, in an attempt to reduce size. In view of some of the traits which subsequently were seen to appear in the Miniature Schnauzer breed, and occasionally do even to this day, it is probable that this is the more likely theory.

What we can be certain of is that the early breeders and fanciers of the then-established Schnauzer wanted to produce a smaller version of the breed, not only for its utilitarian looks and build but, more specifically, for its splendid character and temperament – a breed which had the Schnauzer's looks and ways but, in a smaller package, would be highly desirable to the urban dweller. Over the years, as trends and tastes may change, it should always be remembered that, when breeding Schnauzers, regardless of their size, the paramount consideration is maintaining that very special Schnauzer personality.

THE HISTORY OF THE SCHNAUZER

Given that we accept that the Miniature has indeed been bred down from the Standard Schnauzer, it behoves us to look briefly at the history of the Schnauzer itself. The actual origins of this breed during its creation, towards the end of the nineteenth century in Southern Germany, have never been completely clear, but it is generally accepted that the black Poodle, rough-coated black-and-tan Terrier and Spitz all played a part in the Schnauzer's early development.

What is seldom appreciated by modern fanciers is the close relationship between the Pinscher and Schnauzer breeds. Indeed, the Schnauzer breed actually takes its name from one of its own kind and is believed to be the only breed so to do. At an international show in Hanover in 1879, the winner of the wire-haired Pinscher class was a dog called Schnauzer. This dog achieved immortality some years later when the new breed was named after him, at the time when the smooth and rough-coated Pinschers became two separate breeds – the smooth retaining the name Pinscher and the rough-coated being called Schnauzer.

The noun Pinscher was adopted when the first Pinscher Club was formed in Cologne in 1895, and at the time it referred to both the smooth and the wire-haired dogs. It is thought to have

loosely signified a terrier-type dog. Some fifteen years previously, a breed standard had been drawn up for the smooth-coated Pinscher. This was to prove the prototype Standard for several German breeds which were emerging at the time, rather like the manner in which the original Standard for the Smooth Fox Terrier was used as a template for other Terrier breeds in Britain.

The Schnauzer has always had a reputation for being an excellent watchdog and the fact that he was vocal, rather than directly aggressive, with a seemingly in-built ability to distinguish between friend or foe, made him a popular choice with many dog owners. In the very earliest days reference was made to the breed being an ideal rat-catcher's dog, and to the Schnauzer's distinguishing features, including the quality of his shorter, coarser coat and his facial hair, which was almost beard-like around the muzzle. Also, much was made of the breed's lively nature, friendliness and faithfulness. It was also noted that the ears and tail of the breed were frequently cut. While there may be a degree of speculation as to the breed's exact ancestry, it is certain that, from the earliest days, the character, temperament and utility of the Schnauzer were greatly valued and prized; so, when the Miniature and Giant varieties were developed, these points were the essential ingredients sought in the two new sizes.

The Bavarian Schnauzer Club was founded at Munich in 1901. In 1918 it was combined with the Pinscher Club to form the Pinscher-Schnauzer Club. To this day, this club remains the premier authority, under the Fédération

The Night Watchman with his Schnauzer, erected in Stuttgart in 1620, still stands today.

sturdy and rough-coated dog which proved highly adaptable and able to cope exceedingly well with the many and varied demands that were made of it as a watchdog and drover. These qualities were also recognised, and still further enhanced, by the original small band of American enthusiasts who adopted the breed from the 1930s onwards, ensuring that the essential Schnauzer qualities were recognised and well-engrained in the Miniature Schnauzer long before the breed's popularity really took off.

Originating as it did in central Europe, a recognisable Schnauzer type has been known there for centuries in sculpture and other art forms. It is thought to have been portrayed in works by Albrecht Dürer as far back as 1492, though that may be questionable, I feel. A representation of a dog of Schnauzer type also appears in the tapestry *The Crown of Thorns* produced in 1501 by Lucas Cranach the Elder. In Stuttgart there is a statue, which still stands to this day, of *The Nightwatchman and his Dog,* dated 1602, which clearly depicts a primitive Schnauzer. It is interesting that the first special show for Schnauzers took place in Stuttgart in September 1890.

THE FIRST MINIATURE
The first Miniature Schnauzer to be registered in the Stud Book of the Pinscher-Schnauzer Club was a dog called Jocco Fulda Liliput, born on 6th December 1898. This dog's picture, as an engraving, appears in *Gebrauchsund Luxushunde* (which translates literally as *Luxury Working Dogs*), a book on German breeds which was written by Emil Ilgner and published in 1902.

Cynologique Internationale, for the three varieties of Schnauzer, as well as for Pinschers, Miniature Pinschers and Affenpinschers. It should be remembered that the Pinscher is a distinctive smooth-coated, medium-sized German breed (often erroneously referred to in some countries as the 'Middle Pinscher'). It should not be confused with the Dobermann Pinscher, which was developed later and officially recognised in 1900, and over which the Pinscher-Schnauzer Club has absolutely no jurisdiction.

The Schnauzer was a medium-sized,

Interestingly, this picture shows remarkable similarities to the picture of a dog called Fritzle who is captioned as being an Affenpinscher. This certainly gives credence to the theory that the Affenpinscher played a significant part in the miniaturisation of the Schnauzer. The fact that so many of the early Miniatures were solid black also helps to endorse this idea.

If it is true that a larger Spitz breed had been instrumental in developing the Schnauzer, it is understandable that the Dwarf Spitz (now known in many countries as the Pomeranian) could have been used in advancing the Miniature. Other breeds too may have played their part. At the turn of the century the breed was still very much in its embryonic period, with different crosses being experimented with in an attempt to improve various specific characteristics. The occasional appearance, even today, of a parti-colour puppy in a litter of pedigree Miniature Schnauzers makes the idea that Fox Terriers were used quite believable. Even so, the Breed Standard for the Miniature Pinscher allowed parti-colours as recently as 1924, so that may nullify the Fox Terrier theory. Who knows?

Even as late as the 1920s there was still considerable overlapping between the smaller Pinscher and Schnauzer breeds. Early volumes of the German stud book indicate that, from the same litter, some puppies were registered as Miniature Schnauzers while their siblings were classified as Miniature Pinschers and Affenpinschers – this being in the days when puppies were registered on the basis of their physical characteristics rather than their genealogy.

EMERGENCE OF BLOODLINES

Certain bloodlines had begun to stabilise in the first decade of this century, and a 1907 engraving of Prinz v. Rheinstein clearly shows a dog of excellent Schnauzer type, albeit lacking the heavier furnishings which were later to become fashionable. He is described as "a very sound dog, black with yellow markings". A contemporary of his, Peter v. Westerberg, was, on the other hand, a solid black – and a prolific sire, producing 55 litters by the time he was 12 years old. A Prinz daughter was bred back to her sire to produce the significant Gift Chemnitz-Plauen, described as a black-and-tan. Gift became the foundation sire of Herr Stocke's Chemnitz-Plauen kennel and produced 40 litters.

THE MINIATURE IN THE USA

In the space of ten years 108 Miniature Schnauzers were imported into the USA, mainly from Germany. By 1935 there had been 54 American-bred Champions in the breed, and they all traced back to just ten of the originally imported males and to eleven bitches. The breed really began in earnest in the USA in 1924, when Marie Slattery, of the Marienhof kennel, imported four Miniatures from Rudolph Krappatsch.

Miniatures were introduced to Britain at much about the same time, with America getting in first by just a few years. The breed was given a separate register in the USA in 1926, with both breeds being fostered by the Schnauzer Club of America. Furthermore, both sizes competed in the Working Group until 1927 when Miniatures were moved to the Terrier Group.

During these years, although the Standards and Miniatures were to compete against each other in the same classes, the best of each size had to be declared and both then went forward to the Group. There then followed a brief period, from 1931 to 1933, when the American Kennel Club decreed that a Best Schnauzer had to be decided, and that only one dog could compete in the Group. In 1933 American Kennel Club rules were changed to the effect that a parent club could only cater for one breed.

Thus the Schnauzer Club of America was dissolved and two separate breed clubs were born, the American Miniature Schnauzer Club and The Schnauzer Club of America, the latter catering solely for the Standard variety. Fortunately, by this time the Miniature was so well established that it was perfectly capable of standing on its own four feet, and it quickly progressed without interruption, unlike the situation with the breed in Britain.

MINIATURES IN THE UK
Miniature Schnauzers were first imported into Britain in 1928. Initially they, too, were registered along with the Standards and were not given a separate register until some years later in 1932. In those pioneering days, imports were arriving from both continental Europe and the United States, where the breed was making rapid strides, albeit based on their original European imports. Despite these early imports into Britain by a small number of dedicated enthusiasts, which made the breed's base strong in both quality and numbers, Miniatures, unlike their larger cousin the Standard

Schnauzer, were nowhere nearly as quick to become established and it was not until the mid-1950s that the breed really began to take off. A Miniature Schnauzer Club had been formed in Britain in 1933, ironically just one month before its American counterpart, but it had only a few supporters and for a variety of reasons it only survived for a few short years and was liquidated in 1936.

Strangely the dissolution of the Club occurred just one year after the breed had been allocated its first set of Challenge Certificates, the year in which the Kennel Club had changed the name of the breed to Affenschnauzer – this being the name listed in the Kennel Club Stud Book for that year. However, following protests from the German Club, the breed reverted to the name of Miniature Schnauzer from 1936 onwards.

THE FIRST UK CERTIFICATES
The first Certificates were awarded on 1st May 1935 at the West of England Ladies' Kennel Society, where the judge was Mr F. Butler. His Dog CC winner was the pepper-and-salt, Enstone Cuno, while the triumphant bitch was Enstone Beda, a black, both bred by Mr W.H. Hancock. Cuno was born in April 1933, sired by Enstone Ador von Rheinstolz out of Enstone Barbel von Dingshaus, both imported from Europe. Beda, however, has a far more intriguing pedigree. Her sire was Mr Hancock's home-bred Enstone Erick, a son of Cuno's sire, Ador, out of the imported Enstone Gerti van Duinlust. Beda's dam, however, was Enstone Fanni who had won her way into the 1931 Stud Book as

Ch. Enstone Cito (Enstone Ador V. Rheinstolz ex Dutch Champion Enstone Barbel V Dingshaus). Bred by Mr W. Hancock, owned by Mrs. Humphrey. Born in 1933 and finished in 1936, he was one of the first English Champions.

simply a "Schnauzer", yet she too was by Ador and out of Gerti. Thus Beda was from a full brother-to-sister mating, with parents of what were, technically, two different breeds!

Two further sets of Certificates were awarded to Miniatures in 1935. At the Ladies' Kennel Association show, then held in May, Mr W.L. McCandlish judged. At this show Cuno stood second behind his litter brother, the ultimate Dog CC winner, Enstone Cito – like Cuno a pepper-and-salt. The Bitch Certificate was awarded to Mrs G.A. Simmons' Crowsteps Hilvaria Heinzelmannchen, an imported pepper-and-salt. Mrs Simmons, of the Crowsteps kennel, was responsible for importing several high-quality Miniatures from the Heinzelmannchen kennel in Germany. The third and final Certificates of that important first year were on offer at the Kennel Club's show at Crystal Palace in October, where Mr T. Hamilton-Adams officiated. His winning dog was Cito, who turned the tables again on brother Cuno, while Beda also took her second CC, beating Hilvaria into second place.

Thus 1936 began with the breed boasting one dog and one bitch each with two CCs apiece. There must have been a great sense of anticipation at the Crufts show when the first CCs of the year were awarded by Herr A. Lichtblau. Would Cito or Beda become the breed's first Champion? As it happened, neither won the CC. In males, the pepper-and-salt Crowsteps Hasty took the Certificate, while Hilvaria won her second CC in bitches. Hasty was also owned and bred by Mrs Simmons. He was the offspring of two imports, Major Heinzelmannchen and Crowsteps Holde Heinzelmannchen, Hilvaria's sister, so Herr Lichtblau had evidently judged to type and Mrs Simmons must have been one very happy lady, having won the first ever "double" in the breed.

At the next show, the LKA, in April, Mr N. Dawson judged and the Open Dog class was again a battle between the Enstone brothers. Eventually it was Cito that won, thus becoming the first Champion in the breed in Britain. At the same show Hilvaria also won her title, so becoming the first Champion bitch. The WELKS show followed, judged by Mr

W.J. Nichols. He gave the Dog CC to Enstone Cuno and started off another of Mrs Simmons' imported bitches, Crowsteps Grafin Heinzelmannchen, again a pepper-and-salt, and the result of a full brother-sister mating between Husar (Hilvaria's sire) and Waffe Heinzelmannchen.

The Kennel Club's Crystal Palace show in October saw the well-known judge and author, Mr A. Croxton Smith judge the breed. He was Vice-Chairman of the Kennel Club at the time. His dog winner was the established Champion, Cito, while in bitches he gave a second CC to Grafin. The last show of the year with CCs was the Metropolitan and Essex Canine Society's in November where Mr McCandlish, who had officiated at the LKA the previous year, judged. He gave a second CC to Crowsteps Hasty, and her qualifying Certificate to the bitch, Grafin, thus giving Mrs Simmons another double and another Champion.

One can only imagine what the reaction was to the judging of Herr W. Tschudy at Crufts 1937, the first show of the year. He relegated the dual-ticketed Hasty to second place in Open Dog, giving the class and the CC to Mrs R. Firth's Dorem Domino, a pepper-and-salt by Jeff of Wollaton out of Jill of Wollaton II, imported from his breeder, Miss Dorothy Williams in the United States. He came from imported lines which were rather different from the breeding which had produced the established winners up to that date. History does not relate which bitches were present at the show, but Herr Tschudy chose to withhold the Certificate and no award was made. At

the next show, WELKS, Mr W.J. Phillips gave the CC to Enstone Cuno, which gave him his title, while the already-titled Ch. Beda triumphed in bitches.

Captain H.R. Phipps judged the Kennel Club's show, now relocated to Olympia, and his Dog CC was another for Miss Humphreys' Ch. Enstone Cito. He started off a new bitch, however, in the shape of Enstone Heidi, owned by her breeder, Mr Hancock. She was sired by Ch. Enstone Cuno out of the imported Enstone Gerti van Duinlust, the double grand-dam of Ch. Beda. Unlike Beda, however, Heidi was a pepper-and-salt. Mr W.J. Nichols judged the breed again at the Metropolitan and Essex, where he awarded Heidi her second CC. He found a new male for the CC, in Redenhall Isaiah, owned by Mr R.T. Colbourne and bred by Mrs Langton-Dennis. His sire was Simon of Offley, by an American dog imported from the Marienhof kennel, Porgie of Marienhof, and out of Crowsteps Gretel of Allsworth who, herself, was a daughter of Gretel of Marienhof, so he was arguably the first dog to boast an amount of American breeding to win in Britain. His dam, however, was Bussi of Offley. Now her sire, Enstone Eros, is in the Stud Book as a Schnauzer even though he was full brother to the first Miniature Champion, Enstone Cito. Bussi's dam was Eros' half-sister through Ador, while she was out of Gerti, the double grand-dam of Beda. Isaiah was a pepper-and-salt.

The 1938 season began with Crufts, which maintained the tradition of having a Continental specialist to judge, this time Mynheer N.J. Alblas, whose judging was typically severe. In the Limit and Open classes he only awarded First and Second in Dogs (Ch. Cito gaining the CC with the previous Crufts winner, Dorem Domino, standing second) and First in Bitches (giving Enstone Heidi her second CC). All other awards were withheld. At the next show, WELKS, Ch. Cuno and Ch. Beda added to their CCs under Mr W.J. Phillips, while at the Metropolitan and Essex Ch. Cito bounced back to take the Dog CC. A first CC was awarded to the pepper-and-salt bitch, Quarrydene Gretchen. She was bred and owned by Mrs F. Milsom, sired by Crowsteps Hasty out of Crowsteps Basca, whose dam was bred the same way as Simon of Offley, sire of Redenhall Isaiah, being by the American dog, Porgie of Marienhof out of Crowsteps Gretel of Allsworth.

REGISTRATION NUMBERS

In the four-year period, from the time the breed was first awarded CCs until the outbreak of war in 1939, seven Champions had made their titles. Miniature Schnauzer registrations in 1935 were 34, rising to 46 the next year, but they dropped back to 18 in 1937 and to just 12 in both 1938 and 1939.

In 1946, when specialist Championship shows were resumed after the war, registrations stood at 47, rising to 76 in 1950. By comparison, Standard Schnauzers had 184 registered in 1935, but by 1946 they had dropped to just 56, only a few more than Miniatures. However, they rose again dramatically to 102 in 1950. From then on the position was very much reversed, with Miniatures outnumbering their larger cousins quite significantly, and it is only recently that the Standards have managed to check the downward spiral of both quality and quantity, with new enthusiasts and new bloodlines putting the Standard back on track. In contrast, the Miniatures have consistently forged ahead in numbers, with annual registrations in the UK around the 2,500 mark.

For the last two years of the Great War, a total ban had been placed on dog shows, whereas during the Second World War, enthusiasts were allowed to exhibit at shows held within a 25 mile radius of their home. Although such shows were infrequent, and held on a very restricted basis, they did nonetheless take place and were mainly held in support of the war effort or The Red Cross. They acted as great morale boosters as well as being vehicles which enabled fanciers to pursue their interest in pedigree dogs during those bleak days. While the breed in Britain in the thirties and forties had the Enstone and Crowsteps kennels very much at the helm, in the United States the Marienhof kennel was at the beginning of almost fifty years of great success, both breeding and exhibiting, and it accounted for almost all the early 'firsts' in the breed. Britain and America were working with similar bloodlines, both building on early European imports from kennels such as Heinzelmannchen, with Britain also availing itself of early American imports from the likes of Marienhof and Dorem. Two post-war imports that came from the Continent were Mr Whiteley's uncropped Ch. Chorltonville Quentin Bonus, who played a part in the breed's development and, later, Mr Donald Becker's cropped Dondeau Favorit Heinzelmannchen, who did particularly well through a son, Ch. Dondeau Helios.

THE POST-WAR REVIVAL

The year 1946 saw the return of Championship shows held by specialist breed clubs in Britain, and the Schnauzer Club held two, both in London. At the first, in May, judged by a Schnauzer specialist Mrs D.M. Kavanagh, only Standards had CCs, but at the second show, in December, both Standards and Miniatures had them. However, the judge, the all-rounder Alex Nichols, withheld the Certificates in both sexes, and one imagines that exhibitors were glad to see the return of the general Championship shows in 1947. In that year there was just one set of Challenge Certificates awarded to the breed, at the Schnauzer Club's Championship show, where the judge was the much respected all-rounder Leo Wilson. He withheld the award in Dogs but in Bitches awarded a first CC to Mrs Milsom's Quarrydene Gaynorette, an eight-months-old puppy, who thus became the first post-war Miniature to win a certificate. She became a Champion in 1950.

Towards the end of the 1940s the Redenhalls of Mr Colbourne, and Mrs Milsom's Quarrydenes, were establishing themselves, and they were the main link that bridged the pre and post-war periods in the breed. The last two pre-war Champions to be made up were Mrs Milsom's bitch, Ch. Quarrydene Gretchen, who carried Crowsteps breeding, and Mr Colbourne's dog, Ch. Redenhall Isaiah, with Offley breeding,

German-bred Dondeau Favorit Heinzelmannchen (centre) with daughter Ch. Dondeau Haphazard (finished in 1955) and his son Ch. Dondeau Helios (finished in 1958). Owned by Donald Becker.

Ch. Deltone Delaware (left) and Risepark Ha'penny Breeze. Owned by Peter Newman. Ch. Delaware finished in 1955, the author's first Champion, while Ha'penny Breeze was the first Miniature to carry the Risepark affix.

Photo: Maurice Leusby.

and both also carried Heinzelmannchen in their pedigrees.

Meanwhile a new afficionado of the breed had arrived in the form of Donald Becker. He had brought in stock primarily of Quarrydene and Offley breeding and at the 1948 Scottish Kennel Club show, then held in February, he won both CCs with eight-months-old litter-mates, Quarrydene Gabriel of Dondeau and Quarrydene Gaby of Dondeau. They were bred by Mrs Milsom and became the first post-war Champions in the breed. Their dam, Quarrydene Gelda, produced five Champion offspring, which was to stand as a record for the top-producing dam for more than twenty years. The introduction of Donald Becker's import,

Favorit, who was mentioned earlier, to his breeding programme proved successful and produced four Champions. Mating a Champion bitch, Dondeau Tzigane Lisa, back to Favorit, her sire, resulted in Ch. Dondeau Helios.

The Kennel Club decided to increase the number of general Championship shows, but decrease the number of breed shows in an attempt to make the show calendar more manageable. Consequently there were no specialist shows for Miniatures or Standards. It was therefore decided that Richmond General Championship show would become the club show for the Schnauzer Club of Great Britain. Very conveniently, both Richmond and the breed club shared the same secretary in Mrs Kearns, but Richmond was, in those days, held in July and actually at Richmond, Surrey, and it became customary to have a Continental specialist to judge the Schnauzers there.

As 1951 was the year of the Festival of Britain, the Kennel Club increased the allocation of Challenge Certificates for many breeds but just for the one year, and Miniatures had eight sets on offer. The Richmond show of that year saw Mynheer Heerkens Thijssen, a specialist judge from the Netherlands, judge the breed. His Dog CC winner was Ydrah Quarrydene Gadabout and the winning bitch was Dondeau Howdoo. The Dondeau kennel was really making its presence felt in the early 1950s. In 1951, of the 16 CCs on offer, 11 of them went to Dondeau Miniatures. Furthermore, Dondeau had provided the foundation stock for the rapidly emerging Deltone kennel of Mrs Doreen Crowe, who had already made up Ch. Dondeau Harvestmoon. Between 1948 and 1970 Donald Becker bred or owned some fourteen Champions.

THE TRANSATLANTIC LINK
The first Miniature to be imported from the USA after the war was Minquas Harriet. She was strong in Marienhof blood and, when mated to Pickles of Offley, she produced Ch. Dondeau Hamerica. He sired Ch. Dondeau Hiya Deltone and Ch. Dondeau Harvest-moon, the bitches that were to introduce Mrs Crowe (Deltone) to the breed, and Harvestmoon's brother, Ch. Dondeau Harvest Time. Ch. Hiya was mated to her half-brother, Ch. Harvest Time, and from this came Ch. Deltone Destelle.

Ch. Harvest Moon, on the other hand, was mated to Dondeau Headlight (also from the Ch. Hamerica/Ch. Gaby mating) to produce Deltone Delilah.

By this time Douglas Appleton had imported from the USA Ch. Rannoch Dune Randolph of Appeline, a smart dog who traced back on both sides of his pedigree to USA Ch. Delegate of Ledahof. Randolph was a successful sire and his mating to Deltone Delilah produced Ch. Deltone Appeline Doughboy, bred by Douglas Appleton, owned by Doreen Crowe and handled by Billy Norman. This breeding was to prove the cornerstone of Deltone's success, not only in producing winners for Mrs Crowe herself, but for new young kennels which used Deltone as a foundation. Between 1950 and 1972 the Deltone affix was associated with 18 Champions, while 27 Champions were bred from either a Deltone sire or dam. Doughboy was arguably the first to really stamp his offspring with a consistent and recognisable type and a quality all of their own. The foundations had now been laid for other breeders to establish their own kennels.

Ch. Rannoch Dune Randolph of Appeline only sired a few litters but, primarily through Ch. Deltone Appeline Doughboy, his influence was immeasurable. Furthermore, and perhaps more importantly, he introduced both fanciers and judges of the fifties to the style and showmanship which is inherent in so many American dogs, and which they had hitherto been unaware of. It would be no exaggeration to say that the influence of Doughboy's owner, Mrs Crowe – and that of her handler, Billy Norman – on the breed, through her own breeding programme, and the dominance of Doughboy and his progeny through succeeding generations over two decades, was nothing short of phenomenal.

CH. DELTONE APPELINE DOUGHBOY

Doughboy was bred by Douglas Appleton from his American import, Randolph and Deltone Delilah, a double grand-daughter of Ch. Dondeau Hamerica. He occupies a special place in breed history as it was he who really made the fancy aware of the breed, its potential and possibilities. Doughboy was successful under a wide range of judges at a time when the breed only had eight sets of CCs annually, and there were no prestigious Stakes or sponsored classes, as there are today, to draw attention to a breed or to a specific dog.

Although Doughboy did not always have things all his own way in breed competition, he nevertheless dominated it, both as a competitor and then as a prepotent sire. His influence was equally strong away from the breed, as he was extensively exhibited at all-breed Open shows in and around London and the Home Counties, amassing a most impressive tally of Best in Show wins under most of the top judges of the day. This was at a time when the nation's most respected all-rounders officiated at such shows most weekends, and when the Open show entries were extremely strong in both numbers and quality. It was not unusual for the Any Variety Not Separately Classified Open class (in which Doughboy mainly competed) to contain several of the country's top winning Champions which had not been afraid to travel to compete under the judge of the day and, as the breed classes were more often than not also equally

History in the making: American-bred Schnauzer Ch. Geistvoll Othello of Tamberg and English-bred Miniature Arbey Christingle, (who later won her title) on the day they went Best in Show and Best Puppy in Show respectively at the British Utility Breeds Championship Show 1985.

Photo: Hartley.

strongly contested, the Best in Show line-up would often be a very tough one.

Doughboy was a cornerstone sire and the first really to stamp his progeny with a consistent and recognisable type, emphasising, as he did, the difference between the American and Continental breeding. Doughboy, of mainly American breeding, had a sturdy body, good bone, and a stronger and more typical head (having better balance between the skull and foreface) as well as a much better temperament than that of his Continental-bred opponents which, although better in colour and coat texture, were not so good elsewhere. His extensive use in the breed, and that of his immediate progeny of both sexes, ensured that the breed stayed with a sturdier, more robust type of Miniature that was also good in temperament, a course which has continued to improve over the years with a succession of American imports.

2 CHOOSING A PUPPY

Before you finally decide that the Miniature Schnauzer is the breed for you, do take the time to visit dog shows and talk to breeders, who will be frank and honest with you about the breed. Miniature Schnauzers make excellent companion dogs and require little in the way of special care, other than the maintenance of the coat. If you plan on showing your Miniature, you will need to keep that coat in top form, and few novices are able to do this immediately, so you may well have to visit your puppy's breeder for regular trims until you become sufficiently skillful yourself.

If you are buying a puppy purely as a pet, you may well be offered something from a litter which may not be top-class as far as the show ring goes, but is nonetheless a fit, healthy and attractive specimen of the breed. Perhaps it may be a little on the big side, or have a misplaced tooth, or an eye which is too light in colour – minor details which would prevent it from winning top awards, but which do not affect its ability to be a loving companion. If you

If you are looking for a puppy with show potential, the breeder will help you to make your choice.

The distinctive breed characteristics are already apparent in these nine-week-old puppies.

Photo: Sally Anne Thompson.

are thinking of showing your Miniature, then you will have to look at the puppy through different and more critical eyes.

ASSESSING YOUR PUPPY
First and foremost look for a puppy which is a good doer and enjoys its food. Nothing is more frustrating than a fussy or indifferent feeder – although this would be an unusual characteristic for a Miniature – such a dog will more often than not never quite carry the body or condition that one looks for, and wants, in a top show dog. Some puppies who may be "picky" to start with do, eventually, develop a good appetite, but oftentimes this is too late and the damage is done, as they will have lost bone and substance, so it is important that your puppy has a healthy appetite from the start.

Next comes temperament and attitude. A puppy that is shy or retiring (again untypical of a Miniature), will possibly never quite give one the full confidence

that the bold extrovert will give later, in competition, and it is a fact of life that a dog with minor faults which is a "showing fool" will invariably beat a superior specimen which does not project itself as much in the ring. You should be looking for an outgoing puppy who will cope with all that life has to offer and not be bothered by it. Normal, everyday, home environment plays a big part in giving puppies this first essential confidence, for, no matter how good in quality or beautifully groomed, unless a show dog has the attitude and confidence to show off its good points, it will always be at a disadvantage.

Correct type for the breed in both head and body are two important essentials for success in the show ring. Although ideas of what is correct do vary somewhat, for most people type is simply the overall quality and picture the head gives, along with the dog's outline when in profile. These should be unmistakably those of a Miniature Schnauzer. If the head and outline says "Miniature Schnauzer", splendid! – for this is the fundamental starting point. Everything else is just the icing on the cake and subject to personal preferences in many cases.

Before looking at the puppy in detail, you should study the puppy for the overall impression which it projects and this should be very seriously taken into account. Watch it running around with its siblings and see if it has the noble head carriage which conveys style and arrogance, and also that it looks balanced and totally in proportion, with no one separate part looking out of place with the others. At around eight weeks, a Miniature puppy should look very much in harmony. This is something that is perhaps best appraised in profile, and often, with a young puppy, it is just a matter of catching it for a fleeting moment when something attracts the puppy's interest and it pulls itself together, throwing out an outline which indicates the shape and stamp which the mature adult will develop.

THE PUPPY'S HEAD

Examining the puppies in more detail, the head is perhaps the most important part to consider since it is the most distinguishing feature in any breed, and one that usually forms an important part in most judges' assessment. In a Miniature Schnauzer you want a rectangular, somewhat strong, head with the foreface and skull of equal proportions. The muzzle should be strong with the teeth having a scissor bite, that is one where the top teeth just slightly overlap the lower ones. The

teeth should be large for the size of the dog. There should be a slight stop – that is the angle where the skull meets the foreface – and the planes of the skull and foreface should be parallel. The eyes and ears play an important part in creating the expression that is essentially "Schnauzer". The eyes should be oval in shape, dark in colour and not too deeply set. In the UK, the ears are carried on the side of the head. They should be neat, which means they look right for the head, set high so that the fold is above the line of the top of the skull, and they should be carried forward, tipping to the temple. The heavy or large houndy ears are not called for, neither are those small in size or set on too high, right on the top of the skull. Also easily seen are the ears that stick out from the side of the head, rather than ones that are carried correctly and set forward; and the prick ears which stand fully erect with no fold, causing the ears to tip forward. In North America, the ears are generally cropped (see Chapter 8).

Expression is an important and distinguishing feature in any breed, and results from the combination of several factors, some of which can be aided by clever trimming. In the Miniature we want a quizzical, interested and alert look, not one that is bland, dull or too hard-bitten. You do not want a head that appears to be out of proportion with the body, or one that has a round or bumpy skull. Neither do you want a weak or short muzzle, or a muzzle that lacks fill-in under the eyes, this being caused by a lack of bone and the muzzle "falling away" under the eyes. It is sometimes necessary to investigate this aspect of the head with diligent feeling, as sometimes this failing is not immediately apparent if there is sufficient facial hair to disguise the fact. It is important that the stop is not too prominent, just as the head should neither be narrow or unduly full in the cheek, as both are equally incorrect. All these shortcomings can be clearly felt, if not seen, at an early age, as can the large, round or light eyes or those which are small, too deep set or "beady" looking. All are undesirable.

THE PUPPY'S BODY

Both your eye and hand play an important part when assessing the body and quarters. A young puppy, once it has got up on its feet and developed some muscle, will begin to show its probable movement. By watching, one sees how and where a puppy puts its legs and feet when standing or moving. With the forelegs, you want them straight, strong and well-boned, with the feet neat and tight, turning neither in nor out. The elbows should be close to the body and point directly backwards. Any looseness

here will always adversely affect the movement. Nails should always be kept short, as should the hair between the pads. When feeling the shoulder blades (scapulas), to be correct they should be well laid-back on the ribcage, with some room at the withers, and also meet the upper arm (humerus) at an angle of about 90 degrees. The scapulas and humerus should be of nearly equal length. This will be more apparent as the puppies mature and also come up on their pasterns.

With the Miniature Schnauzer, the angle of 90 degrees is that of a working dog rather than a terrier, and allows the desired forehand extension and stride. When this angle is greater, it gives a more upright shoulder-blade, shorter upper arm and the straighter terrier front. While this may be more elegant in outline, it does make for an unwanted shorter stride. On the move you should be looking for good, forward reach, with the distance between the front legs at the chest virtually the same as between the feet. You do not want to see any

Ch. Amurus Ansome Arry, pictured as a puppy.

short-stepping, strutting or goose-stepping, nor a high-stepping hackney action. A correct forehand is dependent on two important factors – that the bones should be the correct length, and that they should form the correct angles to each other. Any variations from this will be reflected in an incorrect movement, which can be easily seen.

In a Miniature you want to see a good roomy body and big, deep rib cage, with the ribs being carried well back to a short loin or coupling, along with a reasonable breadth of chest to give plenty of lung and heart room, so your puppy should look somewhat "chunky". One does not want a narrow front (forechest). The sternum, or breastbone, should be slightly ahead of the humerus, as a visibly strong breastbone is called for in the Breed Standard, as is a firm, straight topline which has a slight slope from the withers to a high tailset. Beware the puppy that turns both feet, or even one foot, out – they almost always stay that way.

The hindquarters, like the forehand, are also formed by a group of bones all dependent on one another, and, to be correct, the angles and lengths must again complement each other and be in the correct ratio, one to another. It is the hindquarters that give the propulsion and power in movement; so strong, well-built quarters are essential for a good-moving Miniature.

Your eye will tell you a good deal about this area. It is important to remember that the bend of stifle (or angle of the hindquarters) depends on the length of the tibia and fibula in comparison to the thigh bone. A dog that is straight in stifle will be found to

Ch. Brentella Northern Encore (American-bred Ch. Irrenhaus Impact at Risepark ex Brentella Northern Lady): A future Champion and Specialty winner.
Photo: Jean Day.

have bones of equal length. Although not mentioned in the Breed Standard, a short hock gives better overall balance, while a long hock can produce a restricted rear movement that lacks drive and covers little ground. It can also adversely affect the topline, making a dog high in the rear. Also, you do not want to see weak hocks of either kind – that is, when viewed from the rear the hocks turn either inward (cow-hocked) or outward (barrel or open-hocked).

With young puppies it is important to remember that you are looking more at the actual bone placement and

English & Irish Ch. Risepark Here Comes Charlie (American-bred Ch. Irrenhaus Impact at Risepark ex Iccabod Daydreamer at Risepark).
Bred by Peter Newman & Barry Day, owned by Mr & Mrs D.G. Wilkinson.
The first Anglo/Irish Champion, photographed at five months.

Photo: Sally Anne Thompson.

angulation than at the finish of body, as muscle and flesh will increase with age and maturity. With a sound, correct basic bone structure, the movement will naturally improve and strengthen with maturity, but an incorrect basic bone structure will never be improved, either by maturity of body or exercise.

COAT QUALITY
Coat texture and colour in all three major colours are two areas where some knowledge of the breeding and bloodlines behind the puppies would prove helpful in assessing these points and, like most other qualities, they are actually there from the start. In the main, what is there in a puppy is there in an adult, although as far as coat texture is concerned, diligence and regular attention can certainly make a big improvement to the feel of the coat.

Although much can be done in the way of shape by clever trimming and handling, it is important to remember that most judges will form their main opinion of the exhibits when the dog is either moving or standing freely. So, in general, the overall picture and impression the young puppy projects to you, running around or standing as a raw baby will, with the addition of the confidence of maturity gained along the way, be in essence that which it will later project to the judges during its show career.

When looking at a whole litter, you will usually find one or two of the pups catch the eye first, and these often hold the interest on closer examination. What you should be looking for, overall, with the Miniature Schnauzer is a neat, stylish but robust puppy that is balanced and not exaggerated in any way. It should

Ch. Risepark Our Miss Daisy (American-bred Ch. Travelmors U.S. Mail ex Iccabod Daydreamer at Risepark). Bred & owned by Peter Newman & Barry Day. Pup of the Year finalist and Winner of 10 Challenge Certificates and a Group, all before she was 18 months old.

have good bone, a sturdy body and a coat which feels harsh to the touch. You do not want a Miniature puppy to appear in any way "toyish", but neither should it be overly heavy or coarse. Essentially a companion breed, they are sensible and reliable, all of which should be reflected in an outgoing personality.

Finally, always remember that no dog is without its faults, and some dogs have gone on to become great winners despite them, so try not to be overly critical of faults, but assess them in relation to the dog as a whole, and to its virtues, carefully considering the seriousness of any faults in relation to the Breed Standard. Some faults will, of course, count against a show dog more than others, but even those with the most glaring of faults usually have some redeeming features and prove delightful and charming companions.

THE FIRST FEW DAYS

Having obtained your puppy, do please be guided by its breeder, who should have explained in detail the best feeding regime, and given you tips on training and coat maintenance. In addition, you will have been provided with a pedigree, the relevant Kennel Club documentation all duly signed, and a diet sheet. Thus, you will have an idea of what the puppy has been accustomed to and useful guidance for the future. Try not to alter the pup's diet if it is doing well and do not be tempted to give every additive which takes your fancy, as you could be doing more harm than good – especially if your breeder has recommended a complete feed. Miniatures are generally easy to housetrain, and from the start you should give your puppy ample opportunity to empty itself in the garden, especially after meals. Your

An indoor pen will soon be regarded as a safe haven and your puppy wil regard it as his own special place.

Photo: Steve Nash.

puppy should, ideally, be trained to sleep in a dog crate which he will soon come to regard as his "home". Such crates are ideal housetraining aids too, as puppies are reluctant to soil their beds. A crate can also be used for travelling, and over the years will prove a worthwhile investment.

When you take home your new Miniature Schnauzer puppy you will have purchased a devotion and companionship that will be with you for many years to come, for, with care and attention, your puppy should live to a ripe old age. You will have given much thought to the sex of your puppy. Some people have definite ideas as to which they prefer as a companion. It is often said that bitches are more affectionate, whereas dogs are more independent. In truth there are exceptions, as all dogs are individuals. On a practical level, bitches which have not been spayed will come in season every six months or so, and this brings a degree of inconvenience and a period of extra vigilance. While males do not come into season, they can be

equally tiresome when they get a whiff of a neighbouring bitch who is, and this can lead to frustration and occasional anti-social habits. At the end of the day the choice must be yours.

The first few days of a puppy's life in his new home are most important. Give him time to settle in without undue fussing or overdoing things. Remember, puppy has, in all probability, been used to a quiet routine of eating, sleeping and playing with his siblings. The change of home, and all the personal attention, will be a little strange for him at first.

Before puppy joins you, make sure that the garden is secure and totally escape-proof. Also see that you have a bed for him, which should be warm and draught-proof. This should be somewhere that is "his place", where he can go and be undisturbed if he wants to. Respect his wishes and teach any children in the family to do the same. Do not let them tease, tire or over-excite the new puppy. As time goes on, he will want to join in with the family more and more; do remember that puppy is only a baby and should be treated as such. It has been previously mentioned that a dog crate is ideal for travelling and as housing at a dog show, so an ideal puppy bed is a warmly lined, small cardboard box placed inside an adult-sized crate. This will help get the puppy used to his crate from the start.

HOUSETRAINING

Puppies have to relieve themselves often. Right from the start he should be encouraged to be houseclean. He should be put outside regularly, after each meal and drink, on waking, and even after a short daytime nap. When puppy runs around in short circles with his nose close to the ground, this usually means that he wants to empty himself, so pop him straight outside. It is important during these early days of training to stay outside with him until he has performed, as at first he will forget what it was he wanted to do, but once he has performed, give him ample praise and bring him back indoors. He will soon associate going outside with the right thing to do and will let you know, in some way, that he wishes to go outside.

Should an accident happen indoors – and they often do – clean up the spot straight away with a little soda water followed by a touch of white vinegar which will take away any odour. Never scold your puppy if you discover he has made a mess. He will not be able to associate this chastisement with something that happened earlier, and will become confused. If you actually catch him having an accident, a slightly raised voice, followed by placing the puppy outside, is all that is needed. Right from the start, a bowl of fresh, clean water should always be freely available for your puppy.

DIET

Advice about feeding, along with the diet sheet, will have been given to you when you purchased your puppy. This advice should be followed, and the diet should not be changed over-much, especially in the first few weeks of puppy changing homes. Do remember that Miniature Schnauzers like their food – so, do not overfeed. A good guide is to see that your Miniature always has the suggestion of a waistline. Meals should

Meals should be fed at regular times.

Photo: Steve Nash.

always be given at regular times, especially in early puppyhood. Not always on the dot though, as this will only encourage him to become a nuisance as feeding time approaches, or when meal times are delayed for some household reason or another.

Raw vegetables are beneficial and are thoroughly enjoyed. Sweets, chocolate and the like should be avoided at all costs. Indeed, chocolate of some kinds can prove fatal to dogs. There is a wide variety of specially-manufactured treats for dogs which he can enjoy if you need something special for "rewards".

Here are a few generalisations which most people would recommend. From three months of age onwards, three meals should be adequate; from six months two meals are ample, usually morning and evening. From eight months onwards the puppy should be on just one meal a day. Nowadays most breeders and owners find that the tinned and complete foods are excellent and easy and straightforward to use, and they do take all the guesswork out of feeding.

Being a completely balanced diet in themselves, the addition of vitamins and the like is unnecessary, indeed it could be harmful as this can upset the balance. These feeds have also been specially formulated and balanced for use throughout your dog's life, from weaning and puppyhood through to old age. With these foods it is important to follow the manufacturer's instructions and always to ensure that fresh water is available at all times.

VACCINATIONS
Puppies should be protected against disease. The breeder will have given you advice on how to protect puppy against Hard Pad, Distemper, Leptospirosis, Hepatitis and Parvo Virus. Much depends on the products used by your vet, so be guided by him and accept his advice. We are fortunate now that, with a couple or so of inoculations, given when the puppy is around three months old, and an annual booster, a dog will achieve lifetime immunity. There are no ill or after effects from inoculations.

Until puppy has been immunised, and for about ten days afterwards, make sure he does not come into contact with any unprotected dogs. The easiest thing to do is to keep your puppy within the confines of your own house and garden until immunisation is complete. It is often a good idea, after a week or so and once the puppy has settled in, to take him along and introduce him to your vet. He can give the puppy a check-over and advise on the inoculation programme. Although puppy will have been wormed by the breeder, puppies often do need to be wormed again. When puppy is taken for his inoculations your vet can advise on this.

BASIC TRAINING
The time to introduce puppy to the collar and lead will depend on the circumstances. At three months or so, puppy is generally not afraid of anything and will quickly accept the control without much resistance. It is best to put the collar on first, without a lead, and just let the puppy get the feel of it around his neck, still having the freedom to potter around. After a few days of the puppy getting used to the collar, the lead can be attached as you play with him, so that he feels a little tension but nothing

It is a good idea to start training as soon as possible so that your puppy is used to a collar and lead by the time he has completed his vaccinations.

much. As you pull the lead, the puppy will automatically fight it and pull in the opposite direction. With a sharp 'No' release the pressure gently, then start all over again, encouraging puppy and giving-and-taking all the time. In this way, puppy will soon learn to accept control. When you pull him towards you with the 'Come' command, or whatever word you have chosen, reward with a tidbit and he will soon get the hang of things.

At first, when taking puppy out and about, make sure he does not get overtired and drag. If he does, just pick him up and tuck him under your arm for a rest. A harness is not really satisfactory, nor is it to be recommended; neither are some of the heavier collars and leads ideal. By far the best are the thin and round, or narrow and flat collars and

leads. These can be obtained in a variety of materials and colours.

If your puppy is simply to be a companion, once inoculations are over you should enrol in a local socialisation and basic obedience class. This will get him used to other dogs and other breeds, and you and he will learn together the art of sitting, staying etc.

Establish house rules so that your puppy knows what is expected of him.

Should you wish to show your puppy, some of the basic obedience commands such as "sit" may not be that important, as your dog will need to stand rather than sit. In this instance, get to a local ring craft class where the emphasis is on the showing side. Through such classes you will learn how to make the most of your Miniature in the ring, often using food as bait, or some kind of favourite toy as an "attention getter", so that your dog will look keen and attentive at the crucial moment. It is important that your puppy learns to move steadily on a loose lead, and stands in a line, and is not distracted in any way by other dogs.

GROOMING

The Miniature Schnauzer does not shed his coat. With his clean ways he needs little in the way of fussing and excessive grooming. Get puppy used to standing on the table for his grooming; make sure you have a small rubber mat on which he is able to stand firmly and comfortably. A brush and comb at least twice a week should be sufficient to keep him tidy and tangle-free, and will also remove all the

dead, loose hairs until he is ready for his first trim. Do remember to always wipe your puppy's beard clean after he has eaten, particularly if it has been a moist meal. The beard, legs and underparts will need to be washed from time to time, and occasionally an all-over wash will be needed. For these use a good, proprietary dog shampoo, making sure you rinse and dry thoroughly, first rough-drying with a towel and then finishing off with the hair dryer. You will find most dogs will thoroughly enjoy this. If the puppy is to be specially dressed, when he is partly dry, use a cleaning chalk all over. Afterwards brush well and comb, as this will heighten the furnishings and contrast with the body colour and leave the puppy extra pleasant and clean. Make sure you brush out all the chalk and take care that the puppy does not get cold.

Finally, enjoy your puppy and let him enjoy himself. Try and make everything fun. Start as you mean to go on. Let the puppy learn his place and accept your wishes from the first. Be firm, patient, consistent and kind. Puppy will repay

Practise grooming your puppy on a table, just for a few minutes at a time.

Photo: Steve Nash.

The Miniature Schnauzer is a wonderful companion and will soon become an integral part of the family.

your love, care and attention in so many, many ways and will become a most delightful and charming member of your family.

NEW CHALLENGES

Agility is a growing pastime in many countries nowadays, particularly in the UK, since its first public showing at Crufts in 1978. It is a competitive sport, where the aim is to get your dog around a course of equipment as fast as possible and with the least number of faults. Miniature Schnauzers certainly enjoy participating and they make particularly good Agility dogs, being muscular, quick and nimble, as well as being keen to please and quick to learn.

Over the years the breed has enjoyed some outstanding successes at all levels of competition. Agility offers a variety of types of contest, with classes that are graded for the varying abilities of the handlers and their dogs, with the dogs competing against different breeds and cross-breds, but with all of them being of similar size and ability.

TRAINING

Miniature youngsters can begin their training at around nine months of age, with the bigger dogs starting their training at around a year old, although they cannot start competing until they are eighteen months old. Most areas have an Agility Club and there you will receive instructions in the rules of Agility, as well as being able to enjoy practical training. All dogs are individual in their concentration and application, but, for most, attending a training session once a week is enough. Most dogs tend to peak at Agility at between five and seven years of age, but they can continue competing until they are ten, or until they show signs that they have had enough. There is a good and sensible regulation that bitches in season are not even allowed on the show ground.

THE COURSE

Each competitive course is individual and built by the judge presiding over the event. They are never the same from one competition to the next. However, the

*The intelligent
Miniature
Schnauzer can be
trained to
compete in
Agility. Zak goes
through the tyre.*

equipment typically used in Agility competitions consists of a jump, a long jump, a tyre, a tunnel and a collapsible tunnel, weave poles, a dog walk, which is a long raised platform with slopes at each end, the A-frame, which is a wooden framework in the shape of an A, over which the dogs climb, and also a see-saw to explore the dog's natural fear of moving surfaces.

THE COMPETITION
Most shows start between 8:30 and 9:00am and take an hour out for lunch. When competing, it is important to arrive at the shows early enough to give yourself sufficient time to walk the course, or courses. Then, before the start of the class, all competitors have an opportunity to walk the course without their dogs, to familiarise themselves with the order and positioning of the

equipment, which will also enable them to work out the best way to negotiate the course when they compete. Walking and memorising the course is the single most important factor for success in Agility. Before the class starts, the judge will also give a briefing to competitors, with special reference to any non-standard Kennel Club rules that may apply, and also state the course time; this is the time within which the course must be covered for the round to be classed as clear.

COMPETITION CLASSES
Agility classes are governed by the size of the dog.
Midget is for dogs or bitches up to 12ins at the withers. The jumps are set at 12ins.
Mini is for those dogs up to 15ins with jumps set at 15ins.
Midi is for those between 15–17ins with

Zak takes the jump in his stride.

jumps set at 20ins. Standard is for competitors of any size and jumps are set at 30ins.

At the present time there are not many Midget classes scheduled: they are classified as special classes and do not affect a handler's classification in the event of winning one. Similarly, Midi classes were few and also classified as special, but these are being scheduled more now as Agility competitions continue to grow. Most shows only schedule Mini and Standard classes and these have huge entries.

In Agility classes all the available equipment is used but in Jumping classes no contact equipment, such as the A-frame, the see-saw, and the dog walk, is used. With both forms of competition the fastest dog with the least number of faults is the winner.

Classes at Agility contests are separated into six classes, and classification depends on the ability of both the handler and the dogs. These range from elementary through to advanced. The course to be covered also offers a range of possibilities and variations for the type of contest, having such self-explanatory names as Take Your Own Line, Pairs, Knockout, Gamblers and Helter Skelter.

Brett and Alison Roberts run their two Miniatures, Zak and Zen, with excellent results. Zen qualified for the finals at Crufts, which has twenty qualifiers competing, in both 1995 and 1996, coming fifth in the latter year. In 1994 he was fourth in the finals at the Horse of the Year show, which has just nine qualifiers, while Zak qualified for the Crufts finals of 1997 and he is believed to be the only Miniature to have qualified for Crufts in both the breed and in Agility.

3 *TRIMMING AND GROOMING*

The Miniature Schnauzer is one of those breeds that lends itself to good grooming, where the end result will give the satisfaction of a job well done. Good grooming always complements the individual dog and should, wherever possible, minimise any fault. Similarly, clever grooming will always aim to emphasise great virtues. It should never detract from a correct overall picture. However good the grooming may be, though, remember that it is the Miniature underneath that counts. Clever grooming will improve the appearance of any dog, just as poor or careless grooming will minimise the overall qualities of a good one. Nothing, however, can compensate for poor body structure and condition, or for lack of true breed type.

TRIMMING METHODS

There is only one correct pattern for trimming the Miniature Schnauzer. When followed, this will give a neat and balanced overall picture, whether the dog has actually been hand-stripped (which is absolutely necessary for the show ring) or just clippered, which is an easy and straightforward alternative for the family pet. Whichever method is used, the overall effect and look will be basically the same; only the coat texture and colour will vary. If clippers have been used, the coat texture will be softer, the undercoat more abundant and the colour less distinctive and more bland, especially in the pepper and salts. It is natural to strip out the coat because, if it is left to follow its normal cycle, the hair reaches a certain length then dies. When this happens, it does not break off at skin level but falls out from the roots. So, to remove a coat in the most natural way, it is necessary to pull it out from the roots – this is known as hand-stripping. There are two ways of trimming – either the entire-body method, whether by using clippers or hand-stripping, or by stripping in sections, i.e. stripping parts of the dog weekly over a short period of time.

You should be able to appreciate the basics of trimming, and the handling of the tools used, as well as getting a good idea of what the well-groomed

Miniature Schnauzer should look like, and how to achieve it, by watching other experienced groomers working on their dogs and getting them ready at shows, as well as by studying pictures and individual dogs. There is now also an excellent grooming video available.

TRIMMING AND COLOUR
The Miniature Schnauzer is a double-coated breed. That is, they have a soft and dense undercoat which acts as their insulation, and a harsh wiry outer coat which protects against the elements and helps keep them dry. The recognised colours are the most popular pepper and salt, the solid black, and the black and silver; and now, in certain countries where the FCI rules are in force, the solid white colour has recently been accepted. The same basic trim is used for all the colours. Remember that the early puppy coat can often be softish and may bear little resemblance to what the harsh adult texture will actually be.

The distinctive and unique pepper and salt (shades of grey) colouring comes about because each individual hair is banded dark-light-dark, varying from light steel grey through to dark iron grey, all interspersed with solid black, coarse, guard hairs. This is known as an agouti coat pattern. Just as the puppy coat is often softer and less dense than it will be on an adult dog, so the colour will vary from puppyhood, and also from stripping to stripping. Correct and careful hand-stripping will play its part in achieving the correct even colour of the breed. The only way to keep good coat texture and colour is for the coat to be pulled or plucked from the roots. When the coat is cut, not only is the texture

usually lost, but the true pepper and salt colour goes, as does the lovely dense and intense black in both the solid blacks and the black and silvers.

Although the Breed Standard calls for a good dense undercoat, when grooming for the show ring this is virtually all removed, which gives a tighter fitting body coat and a neater and sharper outline, as well as a harsher feel to the coat, as it is mainly all top coat. Removal of the undercoat also enables the body coat to be retained and kept in better order for a little longer than would be the case if the undercoat had been left in. However, it should be remembered that when your Miniature has been completely stripped out and the undercoat removed, so too will its protection against the sun, wet or insects have disappeared, certainly until the new coat has begun to show through.

STARTING YOUNG
Like so many things connected with sensible animal husbandry, successful grooming really begins with familiarity with the procedure being gained from a young age. From early puppyhood there should be regular brushing and combing, as well as attention to the nails, keeping the inside of the ears clean and free from hair, and seeing that the hair between the pads is kept short.

Puppies should be made to stand on a non-slip mat or grooming table and accept the discipline of being brushed and combed from the first, and especially so if they are intended for the show ring. However, early sessions should not be too lengthy, and should always be followed with a game or a juicy titbit, so that the puppy soon associates the rigours of the grooming table with something pleasurable afterwards. Although it should be a period of enjoyment for both dog and owner, firmness with kindness should always be the order of the day, as an unruly or undisciplined puppy quickly becomes an unhappy and ill-disposed adult.

The body coat should be regularly brushed and combed, using a harsh bristle or slicker brush which will remove any dead hair and debris from the skin, and also keep any undercoat in good order. Combing will take any debris out of the beard and furnishings, as well as helping to prevent tangling or knotting. Regular and firm brushing with a good bristle brush will encourage hair growth and aid a healthy skin. Brushing the teeth regularly with a good tartar-preventing mouthwash or paste is something else that should be carried out regularly, as this will help prevent smelly breath and teeth troubles in later life. There will be times when your Miniature Schnauzer becomes grubby and a wash is needed. This can best be done using a mild general shampoo or self-rinse shampoo, whether it is only the tummy and furnishings that need attention, or an all-over affair. After washing and thorough rinsing, first towel-dry then blow-dry the coat with a hair dryer and end with a good brush and comb. The grooming sessions, especially in early puppyhood, should be kind but firm, fun and not confrontational. Your dog should not be kept standing for long periods being groomed so that it becomes bored and irritable. It is far better to spread the work over several days if need be, rather than have one seemingly never-ending session.

TOOLS AND EQUIPMENT

It is always best to invest in quality tools and equipment. They always prove to be worth it in the long run and are the most comfortable and satisfying to work with. If showing is your intention, then you will also need the already-mentioned dog crate and cover, and also a grooming table with a non-slip surface, which is fitted with a removable and adjustable grooming arm. The crate will enable your Miniature to be comfortable and safe in familiar surroundings, whatever the conditions at the show. Travelling crated in the car, the dog will feel similarly safe and comfortable. With the table, getting the right height so that it feels comfortable for you is important. Both the crate and table will be used regularly and come in for a lot of wear and tear over the years, so their quality, lightness and strength will be most important factors to consider when making your investment.

Body brush Good quality, bristle.
Combs Greyhound – metal, two grades of teeth, fine and medium, on the one comb. Used for general combing and furnishings. Flea comb – metal, with fine close teeth. Useful for combing out undercoat and debris from outer coat.
Scissors One pair straight blade (minimum 6 ins). One pair thinning (minimum 30 teeth).
Pin brush Rubber backed with pins.
Slicker brush Another type of pin wire brush and proving to be the more popular. It is excellent for general combing through the furnishings and body coat and also for "padding-out" the furnishings. When choosing this one, select one that is not too big and which

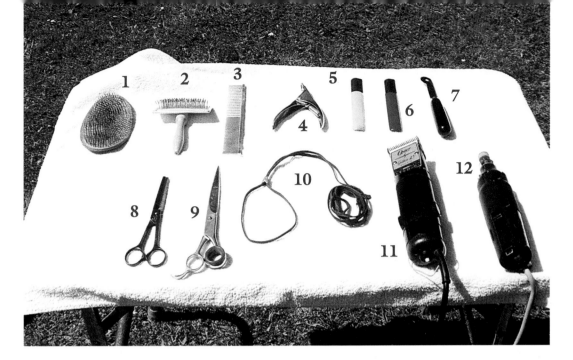

A FULL GROOMING KIT.

1. Rubber-backed pin brush.
2. Handled slicker brush.
3. Greyhound comb with two
  grades of teeth.
4. Guillotine nail-clippers.
5 and 6. Stripping knives.

7. Stripping knife with flat cutting edge.
8. Thinning scissors.
9. Straight-edged scissors.
10. Show lead.
11. Electric clippers.
12. Dremel grinder.

feels comfortable to use, and also look for a brand that has the softer set of pins, as these will be kinder to the coat and especially to the furnishings.

Stripping knives There is a wide selection and choice in these. They also come for either left or right-handed use. It is a matter of finding which you get on with best and feel most comfortable using. It is really a matter of trial and error. One needs at least two knives, one with medium teeth which is ideal for the main body work, and a finer one for the head, ears and chest area, as well as for taking out the undercoat. Now available are a pair of McClellan strippers – yellow for the coarse work and red for the finer. With their slightly turned-up cutting

edge, they are certainly kinder to the dog and do prevent catching the skin. They are also excellent to work with and do give a more even finish.

Electric clippers There is a good range of quality clippers to choose from, particularly ones with sets of blades for fine and coarse cutting, and you should be able to find the best size and weight that handles well and suits you best.

Hand clippers The Hauptner small size (3 cms) still proves popular and easy to use for the close work on ears, cheeks and under the throat as well as on the rear.

Nail clippers Guillotine type.

Dremel grinder This neat, handy-sized motor tool is light and easy to use. It has a small grinder attachment that is splendid for grinding the nails down, and proves an excellent alternative to cutting.

Stripping stone This is particularly useful for removing the soft undercoat fuzz that follows on after all the undercoat has been taken out as part of the show preparation. The fuzz shows through the new incoming coat and using the stripping stone will remove this; but care must be taken as, if it is used fiercely, the coat will burn and the skin can also be grazed.

SHOW PREPARATION

The process of preparing a Miniature Schnauzer for the show ring normally takes twelve weeks before there is a showable coat. But this can vary by a couple of weeks or so either way, depending on the individual coat and the amount of attention given to it. No two dogs grow their coats at exactly the same rate, and often a coat will grow faster after one stripping than after the next. Care must always be taken that the coat is pulled out cleanly, as breaking or cutting can alter both the colour and texture. If you are using a flat stripping knife, then it is advisable to burr the edge to take away some of the sharpness; this will help prevent damaging the coat or hurting the dog's skin, which can sometimes happen with a new sharp knife.

STRIPPING

Two hands are needed when stripping. With your Miniature standing and facing away from you, take hold with the left hand a little in front of the area to be stripped, gripping the dog's skin firmly

The flat cutting edge stripping knife.

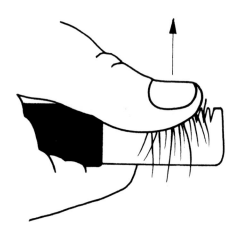

The correct way to use a stripping knife, showing how the hairs are caught between the thumb and the knife.

so that it is held taut. At the same time, the right hand pulls out the hair, either using the stripping knife or the finger and thumb. If you are left-handed, the positions reverse.

When using the stripping knife, hold it perpendicular to the dog, grasping a small amount of hair between the thumb and the knife, then pull in the direction of the lie of the coat, gripping the coat as close to the roots as possible to ensure that it is pulled and not cut. Use an arm-and-elbow pulling movement, not a wrist action, to ensure the coat is pulled out cleanly and smoothly. If hand-stripping, then grasp a small amount of hair between the thumb and index finger, and pull in the direction of the coat, using a flexible wrist action.

If the coat is long, loose and ready to come out (this is referred to as being "blown"), then the stripping will be easy. It is better to work a small area at a time until all the coat has been removed. If the coat is somewhat tighter, then rubbing some chalk into the area to be stripped will make the hair easier to grasp and minimise any discomfort to the dog.

SECTION STRIPPING
This means exactly what it implies – stripping out the dog's coat in sections, with a set-time lapse of a week between each session, and starting with the slower-growing areas first. It is important not to let the time-lapse between each area go on for more than ten days at most, or the blending of the coat later will prove difficult. The following steps should be taken over a six week period:

WEEK ONE: Area covered – the nape of the neck, and the dip behind the withers. On the nape of the neck, strip out an inverted 'V' about an inch wide and starting at the base of the skull to just in front of the withers. Also take out a small area immediately behind the withers. This will give a smooth flow from the neckline into the topline.

WEEK TWO: Area covered – the top of the withers and all of the body and hindquarters. Take out the area of hair remaining at the base of the neck in front of the withers, and all the body coat on the sides and hindquarters as well as most of the hind legs, down to about an inch above the hock. In other words, everything from behind an imaginary line drawn from just behind the elbow to the shoulder. However, leave the hair in the small of the back: this comes out in the next stage, to give a better topline as there is a natural dip here with the spine.

Take care not to strip in to the indentation of the hock, and also leave a

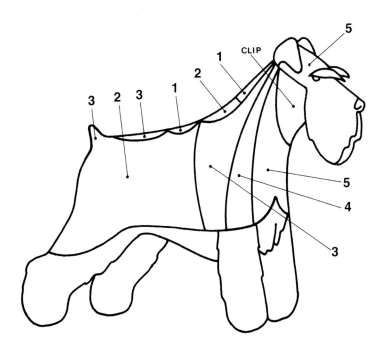

The areas that need to be stripped over the five-week period.

reasonable amount of hair on the thighs, which can then be neatened and blended into the new coat and underline at a later date. Also take care not to strip the hair too fiercely under the chest, as this will also form an important part of the body underline and can be shaped later.

WEEK THREE: Area covered – the small of the back, the tail, part of the side of the neck and the shoulders. Take out the hair left in the small of the back as well as the harsh hair of the tail. Also take out about half of the hair on the side of the neck and shoulders, taking care not to dig in at the elbow as this may give the impression of a faulty front. This area will be trimmed in conjunction with the legs later.

WEEK FOUR: Area covered – the remainder of the hair on the shoulders and neck. Take out all the remaining hair on the side of the neck and shoulders, again taking care around the elbow area.

WEEK FIVE: Area covered – the top of the head, chest and under the throat. Using the clippers, take out the hair under the throat and at the side of the head to the eye. Then, using the stripping knife, blend into the neckline at the sides, and remove all the chest hair to the breastbone, leaving a small inverted 'V' of hair as shown in Figure A. This is then blended with scissors into the legs later.

The whole of the chest and throat can be clippered if preferred, care being needed when blending into the neckline with the stripping knife. The top of the head can also be clippered and, sadly, this is even seen in the show ring; if the head is hand-stripped then the lovely true colour, whether black or pepper and salt, is not lost; neither is the real beauty of the Schnauzer head and expression.

WEEK SIX: Area covered – all the undercoat. It is important that all of the undercoat is removed at this time, right down to the bare skin, and to do this you have several options. One is using the stripping stone, but this can be fierce on the skin at this stage. Alternatively, over a period of two or three weeks, use a flat fine-work stripping knife held flat to the body and using long, sweeping strokes. Otherwise, use a fine-toothed flea comb, again held flat to the body and using long sweeping strokes. Best of all, it can be plucked out with the finger and thumb, using chalk and a noduled finger-stall to give a good grip. This is tedious, but it is highly effective and the most satisfactory for both the dog and the groomer.

THE FURNISHINGS
Before starting any serious grooming of the beard and furnishings, it is advisable to wash, dry and lightly chalk these areas each time. It is not necessary to water-wash and shampoo every time, as using a quick cleaning self-rinse shampoo works well and is easier. During the show period, the head, cheeks, ears, front section and under the tail will need to be stripped or clipped periodically; this is best done a week to ten days before a show. The shoulder area will need occasional blending, using the stripping knife. Remember that the hair between the pads and inside the ears needs to be kept cleaned out at all times.

THE STRIPPING PROCESS
Photos: Steve Nash.

Before the start: The furnishings and under-belly are washed and dried, but not the main body coat.

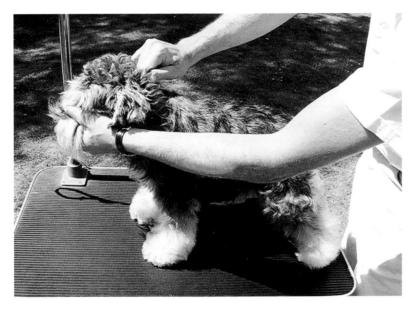

Start work on the nape of the neck and progress downwards in an inverted V.

While stripping, hold the dog steady and the skin taut.

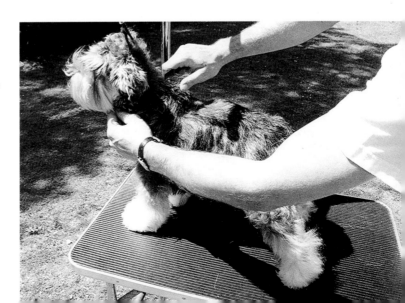

The shape is beginning to come.

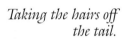
Taking the hairs off the tail.

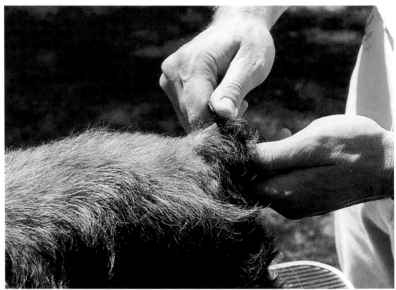

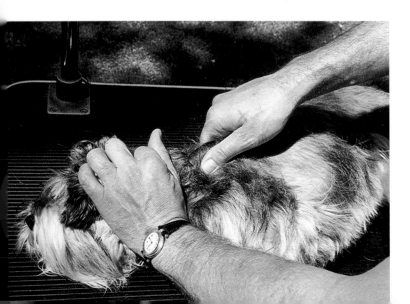

It may be easier to have the dog lying down when stripping the sides with the coarse stripping knife.

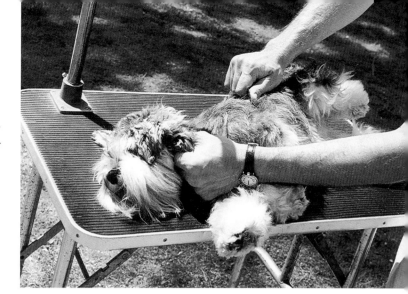

When held correctly, the dog should remain quiet and comfortable.

The dog is standing as work starts coming down from the shoulder.

A sturdy body and a firm topline can now be seen.

ABOVE: The fine stripping knife is used for the head.

ABOVE: The chest area is now stripped.

BELOW: The electric clippers are used on the throat area.

BELOW: The cheeks receive attention.

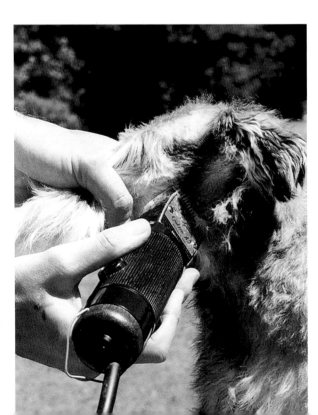

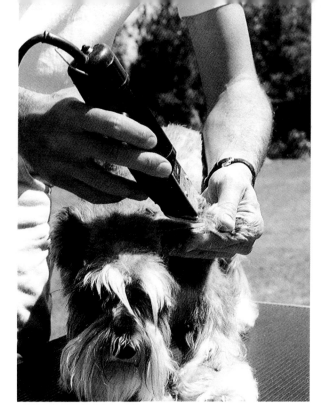

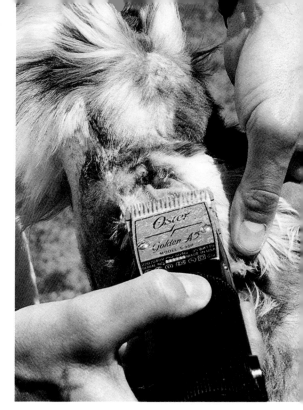

The outside of the ears are clipped (above left). This is followed by clipping the inside of the ears (above right).

Straight-edged scissors are used to trim the ear edges.

A neat finish on the ear.

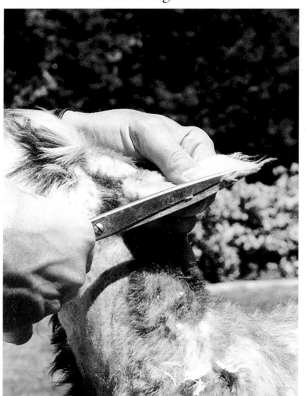

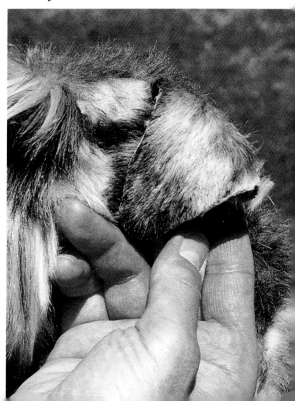

Work starts on the furnishings.

The eyebrows are shaped with the straight scissors.

The side of the beard is shaped.

ABOVE: Using the clippers on the rear end.

ABOVE: The rear end is now clipped, and the hind leg is shaped with scissoring.

BELOW: Shaping the inside of the leg.

BELOW: The hind legs are finished. Be careful not to take too much from the inside of the thighs.

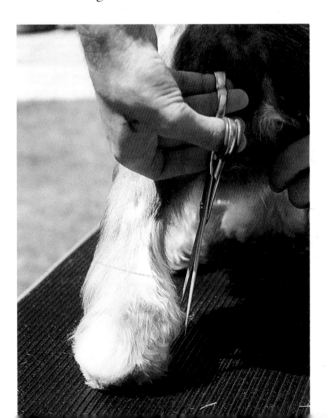

LEFT: *Tidying around the feet.*

RIGHT: *The hair on the hock is flicked up, then shaped with straight scissors.*

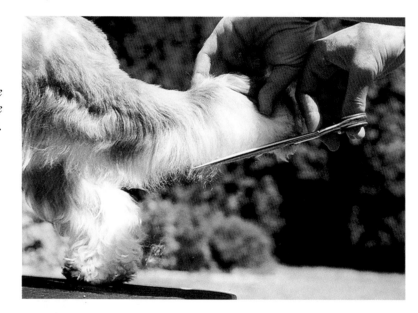

Shaping the curve of the stifle.

The finished shape.

ABOVE: Shaping the front leg.

ABOVE: Take care trimming the elbows.

BELOW: Tidy up the front feet.

BELOW: The finished shape.

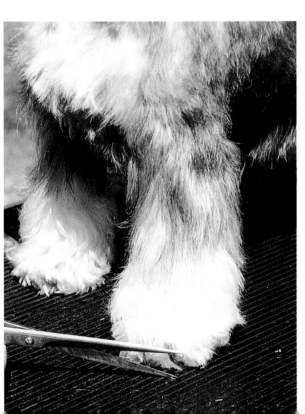

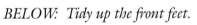

Trimming the underline.

The underline must be blended in with the curve of the stifle.

The aim is to achieve smooth contours.

The nails are clipped.

When using a nail grinder, make sure you wear protective glasses.

Some weeks later: The finished result.

HEAD AND EYEBROWS

It should be borne in mind that a Miniature Schnauzer's head should give the appearance of being brick-shaped, so the trimming should aim to emphasise length, flatness of skull, cleanness of cheeks and a strong muzzle, as well as helping to achieve the correct keen and alert expression for the breed.

Facing the dog, comb the eyebrows forward and then cut them diagonally and outward from the bridge of the nose to the outer corner of the eye. This should be done in one, even, smooth cut. The length of the eyebrows and, to some extent, their width over the eyes will depend on your own dog's individual head and eye properties. If the foreface is short, then a little less eyebrow will give the impression of more length. If the skull is short but the foreface long, leaving the eyebrows slightly longer will help disguise the length of foreface. Should the eyes be light, large or round, cut the outer line of the eyebrows more parallel to the muzzle to give a wider, longer eyebrow and thus reduce the amount of eye immediately visible. With scissors, cut a small inverted 'V' at the inner corner between the eyes and at the base of the stop.

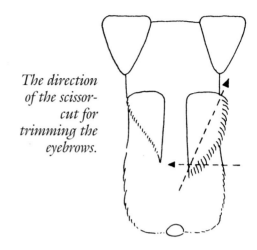

The direction of the scissor-cut for trimming the eyebrows.

The finished result for ears, eyebrows and beard.

BEARD

Facing the dog, comb the beard forward, with a parting on the bridge of the nose. Then cut to the outer corner of the eye in a straight line. Aim for the brick shape so that the head and beard appear rectangular. There should be plenty of fill-in under the eyes, so do not cut or scoop out under them, or this will produce a dug-out, big-eyed effect and completely spoil the whole expression. Do not either clipper or strip the hair on the bridge of the nose; when there is any untidiness, just finger-strip the untidy hairs. In the pepper and salts the dark mask, as the area under the eyes and bridge of the nose is called, is an important feature of the breed and helps to contribute to the correct expression.

Where the clippering of the cheeks and the cutting of the beard meet, the blending should be done with thinning scissors. The grooming of the beard completes and complements the overall effect of the head as well as emphasising the width and strength of the muzzle.

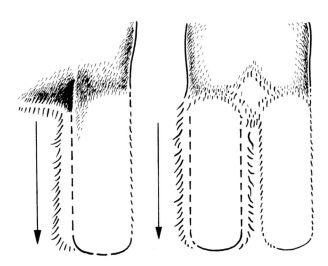

The direction of cut with the scissors on the front legs.

EARS

The ears can be either stripped or clippered with the pepper and salts as there will not be too much colour contrast, except in a few exceptional cases, but with the blacks and black and silvers the ears should only be stripped, as there will be a noticeable colour contrast if clippers are used. Use the straight scissors to neaten and straighten the outer edges of the ears. Miniatures do have hairy ears, and so the hair needs to be removed and the ear-canal kept clean. Because of this the ears should be attended to from an early age. There are excellent ear powders available which give the fingers grip, but, more importantly, have cleansing properties. Just sprinkle a little into the ear-canal and either pluck or use tweezers to remove the hair. While I do not advocate messing about with ears, they can and do get dirty and waxy, and there are good proprietary cleansers on the market to keep them healthy.

Cut out the hair between the pads.

FRONT LEGS

Back-comb the leg hair, then lightly comb downwards and box out the hair with the slicker brush or comb, whichever you find easier. Then, making sure that the dog is standing in its natural show stance, stand directly over the dog and look down the front leg. Using the straight 6ins or 8ins scissors,

pointing straight down, trim in a circular manner all the way round each leg, aiming for a straight-as-a-post look. Cutting the longer, stringy furnishings shorter will make the legs look fuller and neater. With the harsher, more sparse furnishings, these can be improved and made to appear fuller and neatened by a more limited stripping, using the finger and thumb and, if necessary, scissoring any ends to give the final round effect.

The aim in trimming the front legs is to have them looking straight, solid and true from any angle. Take care to avoid creating a pinched-in front or an out-at-elbow effect. A careful study of the front

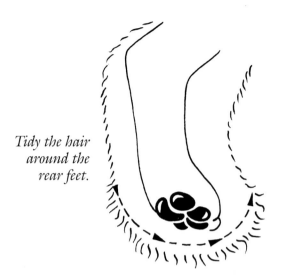

Tidy the hair around the rear feet.

assembly and blending of the furnishings at the elbow, and also in the triangular chest area, will minimise these problems. With trimming the front legs, it is also important to keep them in balance and proportion. The tendency is to leave the furnishings rather fuller than they need to be, which does detract from the overall look – and even more so when the dog moves and they fly all over the place. As we know, once the hair is off, it's off, and it seems to take ages to return; but even so, once you have been bold enough to cut the furnishings down to a better length, the effect and improvement to the leg proportions and the overall balance of the dog, and more often than not an improvement in the way the dog appears to move, is easily seen.

The hair around the feet should be cut in a similar manner to the legs to give a neat, rounded foot rather than a pointed one. Attention should also be paid to the nails and to any hair between the pads, which should be cut out. This will help

to keep the feet nice and tight, and not create the appearance of an open or splayed foot. Also do take care not to cut on top of the toes, but blend that hair into the hair on the lower leg.

CHEST
The blending of this triangle of forechest hair into the front legs can be done either with the straight or the thinning scissors, taking care not to hollow out between the legs or dig in here. The effect to aim for should be a smooth, straight front. Although one wants a good forechest, avoid leaving too much hair and giving a pouter-pigeon appearance.

HINDQUARTERS
With your dog again standing in its natural show stance, the hind legs are trimmed in much the same way as the front legs. The furnishings are back-combed, then lightly combed downwards and boxed with either the comb or the slicker brush. When scissoring, look down from above the dog. With the straight scissors pointing straight down, carefully trim from the top of the hock to the foot in a circular movement, just as with the front legs. Again, the aim is for a straight-as-a-post look to this part of the leg. Trim the hair on the inside of the stifle to blend into the inside of the hock. This will help to give the impression of straight, wide rear movement. Care should be taken not to indent at the upper hock, as this will create the undesirable cow-hocked effect.

At the stifle, the aim will be to curve and cut this line as if it were an extension of an imaginary line that continues the

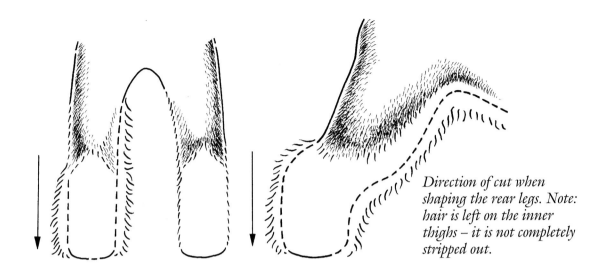

Direction of cut when shaping the rear legs. Note: hair is left on the inner thighs – it is not completely stripped out.

neckline into the stifle, and also carefully to blend the newly growing thigh hair into the stifle furnishings using the fine stripping knife. Again the hair around the hind feet should be trimmed to give a neat, circular effect, taking care not to cut on top of the toes, but blending the hair into the hair of the lower hock, and also cutting the hair clean between the pads.

UNDERBODY FRINGE

The underbody is an area where we see many variations in the trimming line, many of which detract from the correct look and overall balance. The aim here should be to give the chunky look to the body. The Breed Standard calls for a deep chest reaching to at least the height at the elbows, rising slightly to the loins. So the underline should complement this requirement. You do not, therefore, want to see a steep cut-up towards the loin, nor an excessive depth to the underfringe, especially at the elbows. Using the straight scissors, cut the hair under the body from the chest towards the loin in a gently rising line from just below the elbow, a little longer at the chest than at the loin, and here the hair should be gently curved into the hairline of the stifle.

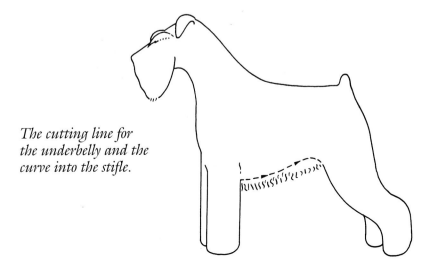

The cutting line for the underbelly and the curve into the stifle.

TAIL AND UNDER TAIL

The area under the tail needs regular attention to keep it neat and tidy. This may be best done with either the clippers or the thinning scissors, taking care always to blend with the rump and rear leg furnishings. Care should also be taken, when tidying around the tail area, not to create a low-set tail appearance or when doing the necessary neatening from time to time. The tail should be rounded at the end, not pointed, and the hair length kept tidy as the new coat grows in. Take care to always trim with the lie of the coat in this area.

ROLLING THE COAT

To keep a show coat going longer, and to extend the showing period on a particular coat, entails considerable effort, patience and time. Flick the coat against the growth with the slicker brush so that it sticks up, then finger-strip the longer hairs from the neck and body, thinning the coat in this way at least weekly. With this regular attention, new coat will be encouraged and will grow continuously. This is called "rolling" the coat, and will enable the show period to be extended, in some cases for a considerable period. It is quite an art, but when done well the outcome is excellent and, perhaps, shows the pepper and salt colouring to best advantage.

Rolling the coat should be started no later than when the dog has been in full coat for a month; it enables a cycle of varying lengths to come into being, but if it is left any longer before rolling commences, the coat will have got too far out of hand to control in this way. The other areas – chest, head, cheeks, ears and rump will also need to be stripped and clippered periodically and the hair blended with a stripping knife to keep the overall picture correct.

BLACK/BLACK AND SILVER COATS

A well groomed black, or black and silver, Miniature Schnauzer in sparkling bloom and condition makes a really eye-catching picture. In order to achieve this, stripping is an absolute must for the show ring, and for the extra smart-looking pet too, as clippering and excessive scissoring will alter the black colour in both the solid blacks and the black and silvers, changing it to a light bluey grey or even a rusty brown. Both blacks and black and silvers are section-stripped in exactly the same sequence as the pepper and salts, with heads and ears also stripped; but for the cheeks, under the tail, and under the throat, the clippers are used. It is important to remove all the undercoat, which can vary in density and colour in both the blacks and the black and silvers, as it is usually not as dark as the harsher top coat.

The black coat needs extra care, especially the beard and furnishings, as their texture will not always stand up to general wear and tear like the other colours, so an occasional conditioning (also applied to the body coat) with a good proprietary coat preparation will make a big difference and keep the hair healthy and in good order. With both colours, when doing the maintenance grooming between a run of shows, it is helpful to strip the chest and furnishings instead of clippering and scissoring, as this will help retain the colour and texture.

The black and silvers do often present their groomers with an additional problem when trimming the inside of the rear legs, as often the black runs into the silver and makes for movement which appears narrower than it actually is, or "hockiness" when seen going away, when in fact the movement is quite acceptable. Trimming and thinning the black and the white inside hairs as short as you dare can be a help, but it needs to be done very carefully.

THE SMART PET

If you have a pet dog that will never be shown, then there is no need to invest in a grooming table. A rubber mat or non-slip surface on a table of a comfortable working height will do just as well, so long as your dog will be able to stand firmly and comfortably and not slip or slide around when being trimmed or groomed. However, you may also find that investing in a simple grooming arm, which can be clamped into place, may be a great help in steadying your pet during grooming sessions.

STRIPPING

Although the pet dog can be hand-stripped in one session (and this is what will happen at the trimming parlour), if you are doing the grooming yourself, then doing it all in one complete session – especially for the beginner – is too long and too tedious for both dog and groomer. So it really makes sense to take several sessions, using the same method as for a show trim, but combining several of the sections together. Doing this will help keep your pet looking smarter longer.

WEEK ONE: Strip all the hair from the body, tail and hindquarters down to

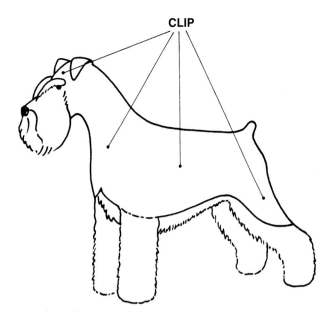

Areas to be clipped in one session.

about one inch above the hocks.
WEEK TWO: Strip all the hair from the neck and shoulders.
WEEK THREE: Strip the head and clipper the ears, cheeks, throat and chest. Scissor and tidy under the tail area.
WEEK FOUR: Shape all the furnishings, and round the feet, and cut the hair between the pads. Cut the nails.
WEEK FIVE: Take out all the undercoat in several short sessions either using the flat of the stripping knife, the close-toothed comb or the stripping stone, or by using finger and thumb.

After stripping the coat and, again, when the undercoat has been removed, a proprietary coat conditioner can be rubbed in to ease the skin and encourage growth. Nowadays they are not all oily and should not mark the carpet or soft furnishings. The period during which your pet may be kept in a tidy, acceptable coat can also be extended by rolling the coat and picking out the longer hairs, at least once weekly, in exactly the same way as for a show coat. The chest, ears, head and under-tail will all also need attention during this period in order to maintain a pleasing overall picture.

CLIPPING

If your Miniature is solely a pet, or its show career has ended, it will be easier to clipper the coat with electric clippers, or by using the larger Hauptner cutter. This will, of course, spoil the texture and make the colour bland, but it is straightforward and can be done in one relatively short session, as well as at times to suit yourself. The pattern followed is exactly the same as that for hand-stripping, so the end result will be satisfactory and pleasing. With the different sizes of clipper heads, hair can always be left on the body, so your pet is neither shaggy nor naked, but can always look neat, tidy and well-groomed.

With your Miniature standing comfortably, and using a coarse-size blade, hold the clipper flat against the skin and clipper with the lie of the hair towards the tail, starting from the base of the skull. By using a smooth, steady movement, 'steps' in the coat should be avoided. The areas clippered with the coarse blade are the neck, body, hindquarters, chest and head. The fine blade is used for the ears, cheeks and under the throat. For finishing and neatening the edge of the ears use the straight scissors. The cheeks are clippered against the grain; this is the only area that is generally clippered in this way, although the head, front and ears may also be similarly treated. The trimming and shaping of the beard, eyebrows, furnishings, and under the tail

are all done in exactly the same way as for a show trim.

GENERAL COMMENTS

When grooming, mistakes are bound to occur, and perhaps the hardest lesson to learn is that, if you make a mistake or create a hole – particularly when stripping or tidying the main coat – or cut too much off an eyebrow or some of the furnishings, then *leave it alone and let it grow out*. Any 'correction' only draws attention to the error and, more often than not, makes matters worse. When mats occur in the furnishings, the best way to deal with them is to gently tease the mat with your fingers and/or the end teeth of the large comb until it has separated as much as possible. Then the remains can be combed, or if necessary, cut out. When cutting a mat, always cut with the points into the mat, never across it as this will cause an unsightly and clearly visible hole.

The art of good grooming is to enhance the dog's good points and to minimise the bad. So, for example, by varying the amount of an area that is stripped in the weekly sessions, even just a little, the effect can be quite dramatic. The weak topline, or bad tailset, could be improved, as could the neckline. Leaving more hair on the flanks and/or the sides of the ribs will give the impression of more body and ribbing, as will not cutting the underline so steeply. If it is cut steeply only in part, this can create the impression of a short body. Making the underline really steep, however, only serves to throw the dog out of balance, giving it an excessive tuck up and an overly "front heavy" look with the hindquarters appearing proportionately weak.

Any corrections effected really need to be done carefully and should be in keeping with the overall balance. If overdone, or badly executed, they only serve to detract and draw attention to the fault, and can even give the impression of a worse fault than actually exists. When grooming, especially for the show ring, it is always better, if in any doubt, to take off less rather than more. Give yourself time to assess your handiwork – more can always be taken off later, but once off it cannot be put back. When assessing your dog, watch him move naturally and show himself off. This will help you appreciate what will need to be done when he is next on the grooming table. Always be aware of his faults as well as his virtues and always trim with these in mind.

After each section of the body coat has been taken out, a light application of oil, or a good proprietary coat product, worked in by hand or with a brush, can be most beneficial, especially if done several times and again when the coat starts to come through. As well as encouraging and conditioning the incoming coat, it will also take out any soreness from your dog's skin at the initial stripping. A quality conditioner should also be applied to the beard, eyebrows and furnishings from time to time, especially during a heavy show period. This will help restore condition and prevent any brittleness and dryness which will cause the furnishings to break.

The tuft of hair around the dog's penis gets wet and smelly with urine. This tuft should be trimmed, but not too close or the dog will get sore. Equally, a bitch is apt to wet the long hair at her rear when she 'squats' and this, too, can become smelly, so tidy here and wash and apply a little talcum powder from time to time.

Your Miniature Schnauzer is unable to tell you when he is in pain or feeling uncomfortable. The regular grooming sessions can be the time you spot any trouble starting, as well as checking that ears are clean, and whether teeth and nails need any attention, so take full advantage of them and be keen to check your dog all over thoroughly.

4 THE BREED STANDARDS

Every breed has its written blueprint, a description of the perfect specimen against which all others should be judged. Such blueprints are known as Breed Standards. They are controlled either by the national governing body (as in the case of The Kennel Club in Britain) or by the parent clubs (as is the case in the United States and Germany). The Fédération Cynologique Internationale (FCI), the co-ordinating body of which many national kennel clubs are members (mainly throughout Europe), generally adopts the Breed Standard which was formulated by the country of origin.

All Breed Standards were drawn up by the founding fathers of the respective breed, and each clause and requirement was originally included for a reason, invariably based on function. It will help your understanding of the Breed Standards if you spend time to think about WHY certain aspects of the Miniature Schnauzer should be as described.

Although the three Breed Standards published for the Miniature (FCI, AKC and KC) are essentially the same, there are dissimilarities which may result in slight differences in the basic types and styles found in the various countries. When judging, one should always adhere to the Standard in force in the country where the show is held.

In this chapter I will look at the three Standards and examine any fundamental differences.

GENERAL APPEARANCE

This is really the most important paragraph of any Breed Standard as it should instantly convey to the reader the "look" of a breed.

KC: Sturdily built, robust, sinewy, nearly square (length of body equal to height at shoulders). Expression keen and attitude alert. Correct conformation is of more importance than colour or other purely "beauty" points.

AKC: The Miniature Schnauzer is a robust, active dog of terrier type,

Ch. Samavi Steps Out (Ch. Iccabod Mixed Herbs ex Malenda Mistletoe). Bred & owned by Mr & Mrs P. Slingsby. Winner of 20 CCs.

Photo: Sally Anne Thompson.

resembling his larger cousin, the Standard Schnauzer, in general appearance, and of an alert, active disposition.
Faults: Type; toyishness, ranginess or coarseness.

FCI: Small, strong, rather thickset than slim, wirehaired, the smaller version of the Standard Schnauzer without dwarf-like (toyish) appearance.

Proportions – square built; nearly square in proportion of body length to height at withers. The length of the head (from tip of nose to occiput) is in proportion to the length of the back (from withers to set on of tail) in a ratio of 1:2.

The General Appearance gives special emphasis to those rather special and general requirements that are essential to the Miniature Schnauzer. These are

American-bred Ch. Irrenhaus Aims to Please Risepark (Am. Ch. Regency's Right on Target ex Am. Ch. Irrenhaus Flight Pattern). Bred by Mrs J. Hicks, owned by Peter Newman. 'Lucy', a most beautiful bitch that came close to fitting the Breed Standard. Photo: Sally Anne Thompson.

further developed and emphasised under the individual headings. It is important to note that the first few words of the UK Breed Standard are *sturdily built, robust, sinewy*, which sum up well the body and simple basic frame of the breed. Although later (under 'Size') too small and toyish dogs not being typical is also stressed, these first earlier few words tell that it is not just a matter of size or toyishness, but it is the frame of the breed that is of importance, so the shallow-bodied, leggy or fine-boned dog is in no way typical of the breed. Neither is the heavy, over-bodied, over-boned Miniature typical. A solid, well-built, sturdy, strong and muscular dog is called for. *Nearly square* is clearly defined: the height at the withers should be roughly equal to the length of the body, which is the distance from the chest to the buttock, and not just from the withers to the tail (this being the back, as detailed in the FCI Standard when comparing

proportionate length of head to back).

In no way should the Miniature Schnauzer be toyish, delicate or have fine bone. Neither raciness nor coarseness are words that should every apply to the overall impression of the breed. When considering the question of correct type, this applies to the dog as a whole, and not to just a difference in the separate parts, such as head or body. It should also be remembered that trimming can create a completely different picture of an individual dog; this should never be confused with a difference in actual type.

While the FCI Standard tends to be specific in proportions in its General Appearance paragraph it does not conjure up the picture of an alert dog with keen expression as do the KC and AKC versions. The American Standard refers to terrier type, which is hardly surprising as in that country the breed is included in the Terrier Group, a matter

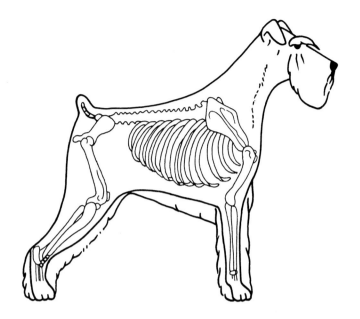

*The correct
skeletal structure.*

which will continue to be a bone of contention in Schnauzer circles elsewhere. While the AKC Standards generally list specific faults, this is no longer the style of the British Standards, which simply include an appended clause saying "Any departure from the foregoing points should be considered a fault and the seriousness with which the fault is regarded should be in exact proportion to its degree" under the heading of "Faults". This gives judges more room to manoeuvre, and can allow personal priorities to be more at variance.

The expression is very much a distinguishing feature of the breed – it is an alert, down-the-nose, interested-in-all-that-is-going-on kind of look. There are many factors which contribute to this – the colour, shape and set of the eye, the shape of the eyebrows and whiskers, the head and muzzle and the set and size of the ears. Emphasis is also given to *correct conformation* being of *more importance* than mere beauty points, reminding breeders and judges that the breed was developed for its sterling qualities of *character* and *sturdiness,* rather than just as a beauty dog.

It is also important to appreciate that, although there is the phrase about colour which appears to limit its importance, it has never been the intention of the breeders to underestimate or downgrade the importance of the unique Schnauzer colouring. The phrase was included in the earliest Breed Standard because then, when the breed was establishing itself, as now, there was the need to emphasise the importance of true type rather than colour or other beauty points. Likewise, in Britain in 1953 when the Breed Standard was being revised, this was just at the time the breed was re-establishing itself, and type versus colour were matters of division when, again, type came out as the winner. It is also interesting to recall that at this time, those who believed the unique colouring was of great importance also held the belief that the dark tiger or donkey stripe down the middle of the back was correct and the hallmark of a true Schnauzer, but this belief is no longer held.

When the most recent standardisation of the Breed Standards, by the Kennel Club and in consultation with the breed clubs, took place, and was then approved in March 1985, the main object was to leave the Standard as unaltered as possible, feeling that it had stood the test of time, and that the Miniature was developing satisfactorily; and so the phrase was still left in to act as a reminder of the breed's naturalness in its origins. It is, perhaps, unfortunate that the UK Standard does not include the words *"resembling in general appearance his larger cousin, the Standard Schnauzer"* which are to be found in almost every other Miniature Schnauzer Breed Standard throughout the world, serving as a constant reminder of the breed's relationship to the Standard and its working background. However, in it its wisdom, the British Kennel Club decided to remove from all Breed Standards any reference whatsoever to another breed – a retrograde step in many instances.

CHARACTERISTICS AND TEMPERAMENT

KC: Well balanced, smart, stylish and adaptable. Temperament – alert, reliable and intelligent. Primarily a companion dog.

AKC: The typical Miniature Schnauzer is alert and spirited, yet obedient to command. He is friendly, intelligent and willing to please. He should never be over-aggressive or timid.
Faults: temperament; shyness or viciousness.

FCI: His traits correspond with those of the Standard Schnauzer and are enhanced by the temperament and the mannerism of the miniature dog. Cleverness, undauntedness, endurance and alertness make the Miniature Schnauzer a pleasant pet as well as a watch and companion dog which can easily be kept in a smaller house (apartment or flat).

The characteristics phrase was introduced into all Breed Standards with the most recent UK Breed Standardisation, and, in conjunction with Temperament, sums up the Miniature Schnauzer well, be it a show dog or family companion. Well balanced means unexaggerated, with all the various parts in harmony with one another. Smart and stylish refers to the way the Miniature carries itself and its overall "sense of importance" look, while its adaptability is one of the breed's most valued characteristics.

Only the FCI Standard stresses the breed's endurance, but in Germany Miniatures are frequently seen competing in other disciplines including endurance tests which, amongst other things, require the dog to run 10 kilometres alongside a bicycle.

The temperament of the Miniature Schnauzer is quite exceptional. Although trimmed out like a terrier, the breed is in no way terrier-like in temperament; neither is it by nature an aggressive or jealous dog. The breed is ideal as a watchdog, being vocal rather than aggressive. Breeders over the years have always given character and temperament a great deal of attention and this is reflected in the majority of Miniatures which prove to be sensible and reliable and ideal as family companions – loving and loyal and in no way subservient.

In Britain the breed is classified in the Utility Group, where the satisfaction and challenge of good grooming may be indulged but where the correct character, temperament and type for the Miniature is not neglected or altered, as it could be were it placed elsewhere.

HEAD AND SKULL

KC: Head strong and of good length, narrowing from ears to eyes and then gradually forward toward end of nose. Upper part of the head (occiput to the base of the forehead) moderately broad between the ears. Flat, creaseless forehead; well muscled but not too strongly developed cheeks. Medium stop to accentuate prominent eyebrows. Powerful muzzle ending in a moderately blunt line, with bristly, stubby moustache and chin whiskers. Ridge of nose straight and running almost parallel to extension of forehead. Nose black with wide nostrils. Lips tight but not overlapping.
Mouth – jaws strong with perfect, regular and complete scissor bite, i.e. the upper teeth closely overlapping the lower teeth and set square to the jaws.

Eyes – medium sized, dark, oval, set forward, with arched bushy eyebrows.
Ears – neat, V-shaped, set high and dropping forward to the temple.

AKC: Strong and rectangular, its width diminishing slightly from ears to eyes, and again to the tip of the nose. The forehead is unwrinkled. The top skull is flat and fairly long. The foreface is parallel to the top skull. The muzzle is strong, in proportion to the skull; it ends in a moderately blunt manner, with thick whiskers which accentuate the rectangular shape of the head.
Faults: head; coarse and cheeky.
The teeth meet in a scissor bite. That is, the upper front teeth overlap the lower front teeth in such a manner that the inner surface of the upper incisors barely touch the outer surface of the lower incisors when the mouth is closed.
Faults: bite; undershot or overshot jaw. Level bite.
The eyes are small, dark brown and deep set. They are oval in appearance and keen in expression.
Faults: eyes; light and or large and prominent in appearance.
When cropped, the ears are identical in shape and length, with pointed tips. They are in balance with the head and not exaggerated in length. They are set high on the skull and carried perpendicularly at the inner edges, with as little bell as possible along the outer edges.
When uncropped, the ears are small and V-shaped, folding close to the skull.

FCI: The skull is strong and elongated, without pronounced occiput. The head is in harmony with the substance of the dog. The forehead is flat and unwrinkled and runs parallel to the ridge of the nose. Stop – the stop is markedly emphasised by the eyebrows. Foreface – nose; the tip of the nose is full and black. The ridge is straight. Muzzle – ends in a moderately blunt wedge. Lips – tight and black. Jaws/Teeth – strong and rounded. A full complement of strong, pure white teeth meeting in a scissor bite. There should be 42 teeth. Jaw muscles – the masseters are strongly developed; however the cheeks should not be protruding to disturb the rectangular shape of the head (with beard). Eyes – of medium size, oval, directed forward, dark and lively. The eyelids are tight. Ears – folded ears, V-shaped, set high and carried symmetrically with the inner sides touching the head, turned forward in the direction of the temples with the parallel folds not surfacing the upper line of the skull. (In countries where as yet no ban on cropping exists, cropped ears must be carried symmetrically in an upright poise.)

Am. Champion Dorem Display.
A head study of one of the breed's most
famous dogs. *Photo: Jausken.*

The head and expression are the most important distinguishing features of the Miniature Schnauzer, the Standard going into much detail as to the ideal. In calling for a *strong, rectangular head*, the emphasis is on strength and balance. The head should be longer than wide, with a flat and creaseless topskull. The proportions have been likened to a common housebrick, the skull and foreface being approximately of equal length. Although calling for a gradual narrowing towards the end of the nose, attention is drawn to the need for a strength of foreface. This also means that there should be some *fill-in* under the eyes, as well as the jaws having sufficient strength and *width* to enable the teeth to be of good size with the correct placement. The Miniature Schnauzer's teeth are large for the size of the dog. With a strong powerful bite, as required in the Breed Standard, there is bound to be some strength of muscle in relation to the cheeks; this is expanded on well in the FCI Standard. The parallel planes of the forehead and ridge of the foreface preclude a dish-face, or an over-emphasis of the stop, as well as a domed or apple head.

It is interesting that the UK Standard also calls for a black nose with wide nostrils, black being a much tougher skin and the full nose encouraging wide airways, which complement the good heart and lung room also required in the breed. One thing that should be remembered, in relation to the head of the Miniature Schnauzer, is that, in wanting an overall balanced dog with a good sturdy body, the head should be, and needs to be, of some strength, length and width in order to complement this, but be in no way coarse.

It is significant that the US Standard calls for a foreface which is *at least* as long as the top skull. This is quite different from a 50-50 head and skull and can lead to overlong forefaces which may give rise to a head which has more of a Terrier pattern.

Medium-sized indicates that large or small eyes are not typical; neither are light-coloured eyes. The term 'oval' means that the eyes should never appear perfectly round, or as slits, nor have an 'oriental' look. *Set forward* indicates that the eye should not be deeply or obliquely set, which would create a totally alien expression.

Only the FCI Standard mentions the fact that the eyelids should be tight, as

Ch. Sonshea Scarlett Streamers at Risepark (English & Irish Ch. Risepark Here Comes Charlie ex Dalylorn Cephius at Sonshea). Bred by Mr & Mrs Dawe, owned by Messrs Newman & Day.
A study of a particularly correct head.
Photo: Sally Anne Thompson.

they should, for a loose eye detracts from the sharpness of expression.

In relation to eyes, both the British and FCI Standards are in agreement, calling for a medium-sized dark eye set forward. This is fundamentally different from what the AKC asks for, which is for a small, dark eye deeply set and keen expression, very much a terrier look,

Maid for Us at Risepark (Ch. Irrenhaus Impact at Risepark ex Champion Irrenhaus Aims to Please Risepark). Bred by Peter Newman, owned by Newman & Day. A head study of 'Pup of the Year' finalist 1988.

Photo: Sally Anne Thompson.

The ears play an important part, not only in creating the desired Schnauzer expression, but also in the overall appearance of the head qualities and outline, the actual ear shape and size having much to do with this. The short and precise UK Standard calls for a *neat* ear. This can be interpreted as well-fitting and in proportion to the head, complementing it. *V-shaped* tells us that a rounded ear is undesirable. *Set high* means that the fold of the ear is above the level of the top skull, although not too high, which would unbalance the head. A houndy or heavy ear is also not to be condoned. *Dropping forward to the temple* gives us the spot to where the natural uncropped ear should fall. The American Standard is similar to the British version when discussing uncropped ears. However, when ears are cropped they must be identical in shape and length with pointed tips. They must be set in balance with the head, avoiding any exaggeration. They must be set high on the skull and carried perpendicularly at the inner edges.

The *texture* of the ear also plays an important part in its appearance and carriage, though this is sadly neglected by the Standards. Too thick an ear creates a rather houndy, dead-pan look, whereas the thin, papery ear leads to undesirable erect, semi-erect or fly-away ears. The UK Standard also leaves out the fact that the Miniature Schnauzer ear has a carriage which is set on the side rather than on top of the head and which, in turn, makes the need for the head to be narrow (and thus untypical) for this type of ear to be in balance and look correct. Taking this a stage further, for the narrow head to look right on the

especially when taken in conjunction with the growing tendency nowadays for American breeders to want a more narrow head and longer foreface than the breed's origins suggest. This, again, is a terrierisation of the head and also of the breed, for once the narrow head is accepted, the next step is for a narrower body also to become accepted, to enable the head and body to stay in balance and, as a result, the very basic Schnauzer look will have been destroyed and lost.

HEAD PROPORTIONS

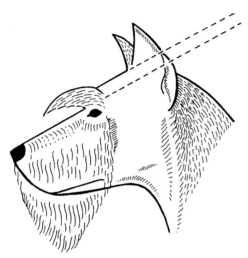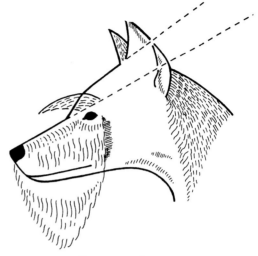

Correct parallel planes.   *Incorrect planes.*

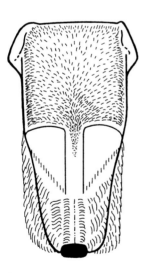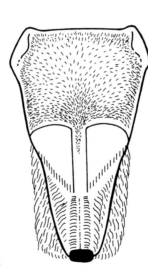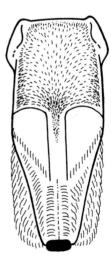

*Correct head
proportions.*

*Incorrect:
Wide skull,
narrow muzzle.*

*Incorrect:
Narrow skull
and muzzle.*

EARS

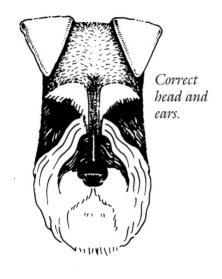

Correct head and ears.

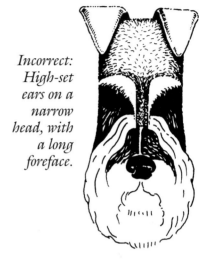

Incorrect: High-set ears on a narrow head, with a long foreface.

Incorrect: Hound ears on a good head.

Incorrect: Domed, thick head, with a short foreface.

neck and body, these would need to be similarly racy (and again untypical). When assessing the Miniature, it should be borne in mind that the breed is a very inquisitive one. Miniature Schnauzers take a great interest in all that goes on, and use their ears a great deal to express their thoughts and feelings. This is very much a part of the breed's natural make-up.

The only correct bite is a *scissor bite* which is clearly defined by all the Standards. An overshot mouth is one where the upper jaw overlaps the bottom jaw and there is a distinct gap between the incisors. This often goes with a

MOUTH

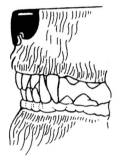

Correct: scissor bite.

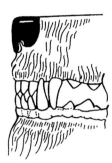
Incorrect: Level bite.

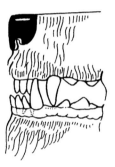
Incorrect: Undershot.

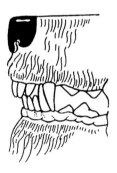
Incorrect: Overshot.

narrow, weak underjaw. The undershot mouth, by contrast, indicates a mouth where the lower jaw protrudes beyond the upper. A level bite occurs when the teeth of the upper and lower jaws meet edge-to-edge fashion. This leads to an early wearing down of the biting edges of the teeth.

The mouth should always have sufficient width for proper tooth placement; the teeth should not be crowded and neither should they be small. The Miniature Schnauzer's teeth are large for the size of the dog. The latest update of the UK Standard now omits to mention the strongly developed fangs, or canine teeth, and that the teeth should be healthy and pure white. Omission of this latter phrase is perhaps understandable, but the strongly developed fangs were there for a definite reason. Omitted, perhaps, now because it was felt to be too strong and picturesque a phrase for the present day in relation to a companion dog, nevertheless its purpose was to emphasise that the breed required good-sized, regular teeth to complement the strong blunt jaw, an essential for the breed in its early days as a vermin catcher.

A *wry jaw* occurs when the upper and lower jaw fail to meet in parallel alignment; it is usually the lower jaw

73

which is affected. Wry jaws are often detectable externally as there is a definite crookedness to the appearance of the foreface. The FCI Standard reminds us of the necessity of having a full complement of 42 teeth, and it is noticeable that European judges place much importance on a full mouth when judging, whereas judges from other countries may be a little forgiving of the occasional missing premolar. In any event, the ideal is 42 healthy teeth, all in the right place.

NECK

KC: Moderately long, strong and slightly arched; skin close to throat; neck set cleanly on shoulders.

AKC: Strong and well arched, blending into the shoulders, and with the skin fitting tightly at the throat.

FCI: Profile – the muscular nape is curved upward. The neck blends harmoniously into the withers. Form – powerfully fitted, yet refined, nobly crested, in proportion to the substance of the dog. Skin – unwrinkled and fitting tightly to the throat (dry neck).

The neck and shoulder are totally interdependent each on the other. Excessive musculation and coarseness is described as "loaded shoulders" and is usually found in dogs which also have a short thick neck and upright shoulder placement. Short necks, with no arch or crest, also tend to produce throatiness, in other words loose skin around the throat, and a loss of flexion at the nape.

A "ewe neck" is quite the opposite of a crested neck, and constitutes a very ugly fault. This occurs when the profile of the neck is concave rather than convex, and appears to sag inwardly. This is often an indication, also, of either poor shoulder placement or inadequate muscle tone. For the neck to be set cleanly on the shoulders, there should be a neckline which flows and blends into the shoulders and backline, with no abrupt break over the withers. In asking for a moderately long neck, strong and slightly arched, the Standard is reaffirming the need for the neck to balance in strength and length the strong head and sturdy body, as well as for it to be in keeping with an overall balanced dog. A neck so arched gives a flexibility to the head, enabling it to be carried high and proudly with the elegant and noble head carriage which is so vital to the breed.

FOREQUARTERS

KC: Shoulders flat and well laid. Forelegs straight when viewed from any angle. Muscles smooth and lithe rather than prominent; bone strong, straight and carried well down to the feet; elbows close to the body and pointing directly backwards.

AKC: Forelegs are straight and parallel when viewed from all sides. They have strong pasterns and good bone. They are separated by a fairly deep brisket which precludes a pinched front. The elbows are close, and the ribs spread gradually from the first rib so as to allow space for the elbows to move close to the body.

Faults – loose elbows.
The sloping shoulders are strongly muscled, yet flat and clean. They are well laid back so that from the side the tips of the shoulder blades are in a nearly vertical line above the elbow. The tips of the blades are placed close together. They slope forward and downward at an angulation which permits the maximum forward extension of the forelegs without binding or effort. Both the shoulder blades and the upper arm are long, permitting depth of chest at the brisket.

FCI: General – the forelegs are constructed as strong supports, they are straight viewed from all sides and stand moderately wide (neither too narrow nor too wide).
Shoulders – the shoulder blade is long, well angulated, lying close and flat. The shoulder is well muscled.
Upper arms – long, well angulated and strongly muscled.
Elbows – close to body.
Forearms – the length of the forearms must correspond with the length of the upper arms. Viewed from all sides they must be straight.
Wrists – these joints may not be broadened.
Pasterns – firm, vertical when viewed from the front and slightly angulated to the ground when seen from the side.
Forefeet – short and round. They have tightly closed, well arched toes (cat's paws), with dark nails and hard, tough pads.

Ideally the shoulder blades should slope, both to the rear and towards each other, and lie flat along the ribs. The top of the shoulder blades should be easily felt and should be closely set, about one inch apart. The scapula (shoulder blade) and humerus (upper arm) should ideally meet at an angle of about 90 degrees, this angulation enabling the dog to move with a good length of stride. If the angle between these bones is greater than this, then the front assembly will be almost straight up and down, with minimal layback of shoulder, and the dog will short-step. Also, unless there is correct angulation in the front assembly, there will be no absorption of the natural jarring which occurs when the feet hit the ground. A correct forehand movement is dependent on two important factors: that there should be correct length in the bones, and that they should form the correct angles with each other. Any imbalance in one or the other produces incorrect action which can be clearly confirmed when the dog is moved.

The requirement for the muscles to be smooth and lithe, rather than prominent, enforces the need for flat shoulders which can never be loaded. Clean shoulders enhance greatly the look of quality in any dog.

By asking for bone which is strong and straight, carried well down to the feet, the Standard is emphasising the need for sturdy supporting limbs which are consistent in their strength of bone all the way down. The FCI Standard dwells on this need for sturdiness, demonstrating again the European insistence on functionability.

Elbows set close to the body and pointing directly backwards tells us that

FOREQUARTERS

Correct front.

Incorrect: Narrow front.

Good front, but bossy shoulders.

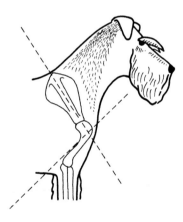

Correct: Clean shoulders with the correct layback.

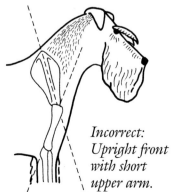

Incorrect: Upright front with short upper arm.

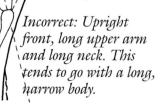

Incorrect: Upright front, long upper arm and long neck. This tends to go with a long, narrow body.

there should be no play in this area, no inward or outward turning of the elbows; unless they are tight and well placed, they can be loose and thrown about when moving. They also preclude barrel ribs in the breed. The AKC Standard is a little more graphic regarding shoulders and the relation of the ribcage to the forehand than is the KC version, whereas the FCI Standard goes into yet further explanatory detail.

BODY

KC: Chest moderately broad, deep, with visible, strong breastbone reaching at least to height of elbows, rising slightly backward to loins. Back strong and straight, slightly higher at shoulder than at hindquarters, with short well-developed loins. Ribs well sprung. Length of body equal to height from top of withers to ground.

AKC: Body short and deep, with the brisket extending at least to the elbows. Ribs are well sprung and deep, extending well back to a short loin. The underbody does not present a tucked-up appearance at the flank. The backline is straight; it declines slightly from the withers to the base of the tail. The withers form the highest point of the body. The overall length from chest to buttocks appears to equal the height at the withers. Faults – chest too broad or shallow in brisket. Hollow or roach back. Tail – set high and carried erect. It is docked only long enough to be clearly visible over the backline of the body when the dog is in proper length of coat. Fault – tail set too low.

FCI: Topline – slightly sloping from withers to croup. Withers – high and clearly defined. Back – short and firm. Loin – the distance from the end of the ribcage to the pelvis is short, giving the impression of a short-coupled dog. Croup – slightly rounded, flowing over into the set-on of tail. Chest – moderately broad, ribs well sprung, in cross-section oval, brisket deep and reaching just below the elbows. The forechest is, through the prosternum clearly extending beyond the shoulder joints, markedly pronounced. Underline and belly – the underchest raises slightly towards the loin. The belly is moderately drawn up. Tail – docked to 3 joints. Harmoniously continuing the slope of the croup and carried slightly raised. (In countries where tail docking is prohibited by law, it can be left in its natural state.)

In requiring a moderately broad and deep chest, the Standard is ensuring that the body has plenty of room for heart and lungs to function properly. Ribs which are well sprung complement this and ensure that the ribs have a flexibility to expand to their maximum. The visible, strong breast bone is not calling for an exaggerated pigeon chest or over-built front, but merely a prosternum which protrudes beyond the forelegs. This enables the forelegs to be set properly under the dog, precluding the straight up-and-down fronts seen in many Terriers. It is this area which can lead to the perception of the American

Profile of an ideal type.

Incorrect: Overdone, heavy type.

Incorrect: Racy type.

Miniature, classified as a Terrier, being somewhat at odds to the European example. This requirement also precludes a narrow and shallow chest. The chest needs to rise backward to the loins, but only gently as there should be ample depth. An exaggerated underline will give an untypical Whippety look.

Ribs which are overly sprung so that they become barrel-like are also untypical and prevent the front legs from fitting close to the body as they should. In such a dog there will be a tendency towards bowed forelegs.

The length of body being equal to the wither height reaffirms the square proportions of the breed, this being all the more marked considering the chest reaches at least to the elbow, giving a 50-50 ratio of chest to leg.

The topline is one area where there can be misunderstanding with the different Standards. The KC version calls for a straight back, slightly higher at the shoulder than the hindquarters. The AKC Standard says much the same. The FCI, however, is specific in asking for a slight slope from withers to croup, but goes on to detail the croup as being slightly rounded and flowing over to the set-on of the tail. It is obvious that there will be a difference in toplines when Europeans highly prize this croup formation whereas other countries seem to advocate a flat croup and high tailset. Faulty toplines include a sway back (which sags) and a roach back (where the spine is obviously convex).

The correct topline should be evident both moving and standing. Short, well-developed loins are imperative in a strong-bodied and well-ribbed Miniature Schnauzer.

The Standards all ask for a high tailset, and yet the FCI version can be confusing, as it also asks for the tailset to continue the slope of the croup. An undocked tail on such a construction will invariably be sabre-like and quite open, whereas the flat-crouped dog with an overly high tailset would probably produce natural tails which are quite curled. It is often the case that a low-set tail goes with insufficient rear angulation.

HINDQUARTERS

KC: Thighs slanting and flat but strongly muscled. Hind legs (upper and lower thighs) at first vertical to the stifle; from stifle to hock in line with the extension of the upper neck line; from hock vertical to ground. Feet – short, round, cat-like, compact with closely arched toes, dark nails, firm black pads, feet pointing forwards.

AKC: The hindquarters have strong-muscled slanting thighs, they are well bent at the stifles. There is sufficient angulation so that, in stance, the hocks extend beyond the tail. The hindquarters never appear overbuilt or higher than the shoulders. The rear pasterns are short and, in stance, perpendicular to the ground and when viewed from the rear are parallel to each other. Feet – short and round (cat feet) with thick, black pads. The toes are arched and compact.

FCI: General – seen from the side they are slanting, viewed from behind parallel.
Upper thighs – long, in harmony with the substance of the dog, directed forward, broad and strongly muscled.
Knee – clearly angulated, is situated straight between the upper and under thigh, without pointing inward nor outward.
Under thighs – long and strong, length in correct proportion to the whole build of the hindquarters.
Hock joint – angulation well pronounced.
Rear pasterns – longer than the front pasterns, yet not too long, not disturbing the harmony.
Hind feet – as forefeet, only longer. No rear dewclaws.

The hindquarters, like the fore, are formed by a group of bones all interdependent on one another. In order for them to have the correct angulation and produce the correct movement, the bone lengths and angles must complement each other, as well as being in the correct ratio to one another; otherwise narrow, straight hindquarters lacking power will be the result. It is mainly the hindquarters that give the propulsion for movement. Correct angulation and muscle tone ensures that the propulsion is strong and powerful, and that it is absorbed correctly through the body; also that the whole dog moves forward efficiently.

A lack of angulation will mean that the propulsion is pushed upwards rather than forward. Although the hindquarters should be well developed and strongly muscled, thighs slanting and flat means that they should not be overmuscled, as those in some of the running breeds

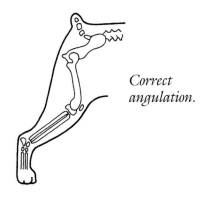

Correct angulation.

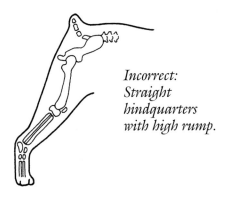

Incorrect: Straight hindquarters with high rump.

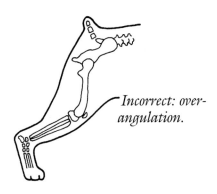

Incorrect: over-angulation.

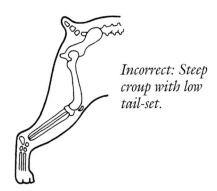

Incorrect: Steep croup with low tail-set.

tend to be. Neither should the hindquarters be so wide that the dog double-tracks when moving, which means the rear legs move outside the track of the front legs.

The requirement for the rear angulation to be in line with the upper neckline is very helpful in assessing balance in a Miniature Schnauzer. Think of an imaginary line extending down from the upper neckline and passing through the withers which should join with the angulation of the lower hind leg. This also ensures that the propulsion effort is at its most effective and is absorbed evenly throughout the body, with no particular joint having any more wear and tear or jarring than any other.

A short hock creates a better overall balance to the dog, while a long hock can play a part in producing restricted rear movement that lacks drive and covers little ground. It can also have an adverse effect on the topline, making it high behind. A weak hock which turns either in (cow hocks) or out (open or barrel hocks) can often also be seen and neither can ever produce efficient rear movement.

The toes are arched and compact, with the two centre toes only just slightly forward of the others. Firm, black pads ensure that the feet are able to cope with varied ground conditions. Black pigment helps towards a tough skin. Incorrect foot types sometimes seen in Miniatures include hare feet (flat and long) and splayed feet (when the toes are spread out). Pasterns should only be slightly bent and springy, and thus be able to satisfactorily absorb any shock created by movement. Upright pasterns can cause a dog to knuckle over at the knee. This is a bad fault, but one that is easily visible, even though the breed has leg furnishings. Weak pasterns may allow the feet to point either inwards or outwards. The nails should be kept short and thus help to maintain neat, tight feet. The required dark nails go hand in hand with strong pigment.

GAIT/MOVEMENT

KC: Free, balanced and vigorous, with good reach in forequarters and good driving power in hindquarters. Topline remains level in action.

AKC: The trot is the gait at which movement is judged. When approaching, the forelegs, with elbows close to the body, move straight forward, neither too close nor too far apart. Going away, the hind legs are straight and travel in the same planes as the forelegs.
Note: It is generally accepted that when a full trot is achieved, the rear legs continue to move in the same planes as the forelegs, but a very slight inward inclination will occur. It begins at the point of the shoulder in front and at the hip joint at the rear. Viewed from front or rear, the legs are straight from these points to the pads. The degree of inward inclination is almost imperceptible in a Miniature Schnauzer that has correct movement. It does not justify moving close, toeing in, crossing or moving out at the elbows.
Viewed from the side, the forelegs have good reach, while the hind legs have strong drive, with good pick up of hocks. The feet turn neither inward nor outward.
Faults: Single tracking, side gaiting, paddling in front, or hackney action. Weak rear action.

FCI: Dogs move in three different ways: walk, trot and gallop. When on the lead the dog will normally walk, although the most frequent

MOVEMENT

Correct movement in profile.

Incorrect: Short stride with no ground coverage.

movement is the trot. Gallop is
possible. Walk and trot have to be
performed in diagonal sequence.
Typical for the trot is an ample
ground-covering, free and smooth
movement, with powerful drive from
the rear and good reach in the front.
Viewed from the rear or the front, the
legs move in straight lines.

Movement is a major consideration
when judging any breed, as it is an
unquestionable indication of structure,
balance, soundness, temperament and
"style" if studied knowledgeably. A
badly-made dog will never move
correctly, though a well made dog can
sometimes move less than ideally if
having an "off" day, or when it is being
badly handled and shown.

Proper movement requires correct
structure and muscle co-ordination. The
Miniature Schnauzer should have a
balanced, free-flowing, easy and
rhythmic movement. It should never be
stiff or stilted, nor lacking in power and
rear drive. The forelegs should always
exhibit good reach and move in two
parallel planes (though, as the AKC
Standard explains in detail, an increase in
speed at the trot will result in the legs
converging to a slight degree), the
distance between the elbows and
between the feet being the same. The
elbows must be close to the body. Hocks
should be parallel and drawn under the
body when moving, so that the body is
pushed off with some force, producing a
powerful, driving motion. Any deviation,
inside or outside these parallel lines, is a
fault.

Explanation of "diagonal sequence" is
simply that correct and economic action

occurs when the left foreleg and right
hindleg move forward at the same time,
followed by the right foreleg and the left
hind. Frequently seen is a lazy action,
often resulting from faulty conformation
(though it must be said, this can be
habitual, in which case the offending
dog should be trained out of it), known
as "pacing" when the right foreleg and
right hind move forward at the same
time, followed by the left legs.

It is interesting that only the KC
Standard mentions topline in the gait
section of the Standard, as this is an
important aspect of overall carriage and
one to which American judges,
particularly, pay great attention.

A dog which is correctly made, and
moves correctly, should go away with
such strength and drive that it clearly
shows the soles of its rear pads when
"kicking off".

COAT AND COLOUR

**KC: Harsh, wiry, and short enough
for smartness, dense undercoat. Clean
on neck and shoulders, ears and skull.
Harsh hair on legs. Furnishings fairly
thick but not silky.
All pepper and salt colours in even
proportions, or pure black, or black
and silver. That is, solid black with
silver markings on eyebrows, muzzle,
chest and brisket and on the forelegs
below the point of elbow, on inside of
hindlegs below the stifle joint, on
vent and under tail.**

**AKC: Double, with hard, wiry outer
coat and close undercoat. The head,
neck, ears, chest, tail and body coat
must be plucked. When in show**

condition, the body coat should be of sufficient length to determine texture. Close covering on neck, ears and skull. Furnishings are fairly thick but not silky.

Faults: Coat too soft or too smooth and slick in appearance.

The recognized colors are salt and pepper, black and silver, and solid black. All colors have uniform skin pigmentation, i.e. no white or pink skin patches shall appear anywhere on the dog.

Salt and pepper: The typical salt and pepper color of the top coat results from the combination of black and white banded hairs and solid black and solid white unbanded hairs, with the banded hairs predominating. Acceptable are all shades of salt and pepper from light to dark mixtures with tan shading permissible in the banded or unbanded hair of the top coat. In salt and pepper dogs, the salt and pepper mixture fades out to light gray or silver white in the eyebrows, whiskers, cheeks, underthroat, inside the ears, across chest, under tail, leg furnishings, and inside hind legs. It may or may not fade out on the underbody. However, if so, the lighter underbody hair is not to rise higher on the sides of the body than the front elbows.

Black and silver: The black and silver generally follows the same pattern as the salt and pepper. The entire salt and pepper section must be black. The black color in the top coat of the black and silver is a true, rich color with black undercoat. The stripped portion is free from any fading or brown tinge and the underbody should be dark.

Black: Black is the only solid color allowed. Ideally the black color in the top coat is a true, rich, glossy solid color with the undercoat being less intense, a soft matt shade of black. This is natural and should not be penalised in any way. The stripped portion is free from any fading or brown tinge. The scissored and clippered areas have lighter shades of black. A small white spot on the chest is permitted, as is an occasional single white hair elsewhere on the body.

Disqualifications: Color solid white or white striping, patching or spotting on the colored areas of the dog, except for a small white spot on the chest of the black. The body coat color in salt and pepper and black and silver dogs fades out to light gray or silver white under the throat and across the chest. Between them there exists a natural body coat color. Any irregular or connecting blaze or white mark in this section is considered a white patch on the body which is also a disqualification.

FCI: Skin tight fitting over the whole body (dry skin). The black dogs have a medium grey skin, the pepper and salt has a lighter pigmentation, in black and silver medium grey, and in white as dark as possible.

The coat is wirehaired. It should be wiry and close. It consists of a thick undercoat and a hard, flat-lying top coat, which under no circumstances should be too short. The top coat is wiry, never shaggy or wavy. The hair at the head and the legs is also harsh, on the forehead and the ears slightly shorter. The typical hallmarks are a not too soft beard and the bushy eyebrows which slightly overshadow the eyes.

Colour: a) Solid black with black undercoat. b) Pepper and salt. c) Black and silver. d) Pure white with white undercoat.

The breeding aim for the pepper and salt colour is a medium shade, with an evenly distributed and intensely pigmented "peppering", and a grey undercoat. Admissible are the shades ranging from dark iron-grey to silver-grey. All shades must have a dark mask which harmoniously fits the particular shade and emphasises the expression. Lighter markings on the head, chest and legs are undesirable. The breeding aim for the black and silver Miniature Schnauzer is a black top coat with a black undercoat; with white markings above the eyes, on the throat, on the cheeks, on the front part of the chest two separate triangles, on the front pasterns, on the paws, on the inside of the hindquarters and under the tail. Forehead, neck and outside of ears should, like the top coat, be black.

The Miniature Schnauzer has a double coat which is a hard, wiry outer coat and a dense but softer undercoat. The hard outer coat acts as protection against the elements while the undercoat serves as insulation. Hand stripping helps retain the good coat texture, as well as the correct and unique pepper and salt colouring. Clipping will spoil the ideal texture and can also lead to a loss of colour and the appearance of a brownish hue.

Furnishings should be fairly thick and dense, but will not be as harsh as the body coat. They should not be silky in texture. In reality, Miniature Schnauzers shown in the FCI countries tend to have much harsher and sparser leg furnishings, while the Americans have more profuse leg hair. Britain lies, as it does geographically, somewhere in the middle.

Although some harsh coats may have a slight wave, especially when the coat is long, coats of proper texture never curl, even when wet. An open coat does not fit the body tightly. A single coat has no undercoat. The coat should always be short enough for smartness, but it should never be so short that the dog

Salt and pepper: Spanish Ch. Malenda Mixed Mints, bred in the UK.

Black and silver: Ch. Scedir don Fdelio, Ch. Scedir Pablo Picasso, Ch. Scedir Mister X, Ch. Sedir Xantippe, and Ch. Scedir Twiggy, bred in Italy.

looks scalped or heavily barbered. The coat texture should always be clearly visible and is vital to the overall look of robustness.

The coat should always be properly blended from one area to the next and, although shorter on skull, ears, neck and shoulder, it should still always show the correct colour. Although the Standards all require a dense undercoat, if this is allowed to grow unchecked, it quickly spoils the body contour and the well-groomed look, as well as detracting from the harsh texture of the outer coat.

The FCI Standard mention of the tight-fitting skin is something which the other Standards could well have adopted, as this quality is essential to the overall look of the breed. A Miniature with loose skin on its throat or body will look soft and sloppy, and can never have

that clean, sharp outline which is so very much part of the breed's charm.

On colour there is obvious disagreement over what is acceptable now that the FCI has admitted pure white Miniatures to the register. Neither the KC nor the AKC accept this colour, and it is still the feeling of some Schnauzer breeders in these countries that the white colouring has only been established through the introduction of other breeds, so they question the purity of such specimens. However, when judging under FCI rules, the whites are perfectly acceptable and must be judged accordingly.

The distinctive pepper and salt colour in the breed is unique and is due to the fact that each hair of the harsh outer coat is banded by three bands of light and dark shades of grey. This is known as the

Black: Ocus Pocus vd Havenstad, bred and owned by C de Meulenaer in Belgium.

agouti coat pattern. The colour variation seen between light and dark dogs comes about through the ratio of light to dark colours; the banding, and the depth of colour, as well as the length of banding on each hair, all playing an important part. The dark dogs have the majority of the hair ends dark, while in the lighter coloured dogs there are more lighter ends. Often the coat will change colour from stripping to stripping, or with the changing climatic seasons. "Even proportions" means that each hair should be banded, rather than just some, which would produce a blotchy effect.

Correct trimming also plays an important part in achieving the correct, even-colour effect. A head that is stripped rather than clippered will noticeably reflect this, particularly in expression. The main pepper and salt colour fades out to a lighter grey or silvery white in the leg furnishings, eyebrows, beard, cheeks, under the tail, under the body and inside the hind legs.

It is important that this lighter hair should not rise higher on the sides of the body than the front elbows; neither should it invade the thigh area of the hindquarters. The black and silver follows the same pattern as that of the pepper and salt, except that the entire pepper and salt section must be pure black with no white, red or grey hairs intermingled in the body colour.

Black is the only solid colour permitted by the KC and AKC and it should be a pure black, again with no white, grey or red hairs intermingled. A small white breast spot is, however, permitted. In blacks, the whiskers may become discoloured with time and show a slight red tinge. With the pepper and salts, yellow, tan, red or cream are sometimes seen in the main body colours which are not correct. This should not be confused with the few red hairs that are sometimes seen at the nape of the neck. The hair on the bridge of the nose should always be darker than the body colour, and this is still referred to as the dark mask in the FCI Standard.

SIZE AND WEIGHT

KC: The ideal height for dogs should be 35.6 cms (14 inches) and for bitches 33 cms (13 inches). Too small, toyish-appearing dogs are not typical and are undesirable.

AKC: From 12 to 14 inches. He is sturdily built, nearly square in proportion of body length to height with plenty of bone, and without any suggestion of toyishness. Disqualifications: Dogs or bitches under 12 inches or over 14 inches.

FCI: Height at withers: For dogs and bitches between 30 and 35 cm. Weight: For dogs and bitches between 4 to 6 kg.

The height should be measured at the withers. While height limits are important, especially in breeds like the Schnauzer family where there is more than one size, it should always be borne in mind that well-boned, well-coated dogs will usually appear larger than their lighter-boned and shorter-coated counterparts. Quality and balance are essential requirements, and it is perhaps to the detriment of the breed that the AKC Standard lists over and under size as disqualifications. This could rob the breed of an outstanding specimen which is "just" over the limit.

As I have said, the KC Standards for all breeds no longer list any disqualifying faults, apart from the Miniature

Dachshund varieties and the Toy and Miniature Poodle varieties where dogs must weigh or measure "in" before being awarded a prize card. Other breeds, the Miniature Schnauzer included, simply have appended at the end of the Breed Standard the sentence: "Any departure from the foregoing points should be considered a fault and the seriousness with which the fault should be regarded should be in exact proportion to its degree." This is a fair and wise directive.

AKC disqualifies monorchid cryptorchid males, whereas these can be exhibited in Britain. Debating the wisdom of this ruling would take up a book in itself!

The FCI Standard lists the following disqualifications:
1. Deformities of any kind.
2. Monorchids or cryptorchids. Dogs must have two clearly normal developed testicles, fully descended in the scrotum.
3. Insufficient type.
4. Overshot, undershot, or more than two missing teeth.
5. Severe faults in specific parts of the anatomy, coat and colour.
6. Shy or vicious attitude.

Disqualifying faults are normally specific in nature, but the FCI list includes some rather vague shortcomings. There is every possibility that this could lead to rather inconsistent judging, as what one judge may view as "insufficient type" could be seen as quite acceptable by another. In this respect, I believe the British Standard deals with faults in the best and most logical fashion.

5 SHOWING YOUR MINIATURE SCHNAUZER

Assuming that your Miniature Schnauzer puppy or youngster has been sensibly brought up and well reared, and its coat well maintained, there should be no real problems should you decide to venture into the show ring. That is, provided your dog is a typical example of the breed which fulfils the basic requirements of the Breed Standard. Should you decide to show, you will obviously need to attend some kind of training classes where both you and your future show dog will learn the ropes; and remember that when you turn up at the first of these sessions, your dog will be finding itself in a completely new situation. Some dogs will cope and adjust more quickly than others, so care and patience should be the order of the day.

THE PLEASURES OF SHOWING
There is a great deal of pleasure to be derived from showing a well-bred dog, who has been beautifully groomed and trained for the show ring. Whether he wins or not, the important factor is to have him looking his very best so that he

is a credit to both you and his breeding. Showing is not as easy as it might first appear; a great deal of work and effort goes into having an exhibit looking and showing to such a degree that it all appears completely natural and effortless.

We become involved in showing dogs for many and varied reasons. Once committed, however, a whole new interest opens up with the dog world. We all meet on equal terms and share a common interest – the love of our breed and the "dog game". The breeding and exhibiting of pure-bred dogs is a tremendously challenging sport and has much to offer, particularly in fellowship, good sportsmanship and competitiveness. It also offers enjoyment and involvement for the whole family. It is a world-wide sport and interest that takes no notice of national barriers, class, colour or creed. It creates friendships that endure a lifetime. The backbone of any breed is the serious breeders and their willingness to compete regularly at the shows against one another, thus enabling them to evaluate the progress and development of their own breeding programme. It is the desire to monitor the relative quality of the breeders' emerging stock which first brought dog shows into being. Today, however, there are far more "hobby exhibitors" supporting the fancy than large-scale breeders, and the fact that they, too, can reach the highest heights says much for the openness of the dog-showing world. Great dogs – whoever might own them – are more often made through competition and the subsequent success of their progeny, not by just staying at home.

UK COMPETITIONS

In Britain there are several types of competitions. At the lower end of the scale are the Exemption Shows. Although they need to be licensed by the Kennel Club, these are essentially "fun" events where dogs can be entered on the day and the classification includes classes for pedigree and non-pedigree dogs. They are invariably run in aid of a local or national charity, or other good cause, and are often held in conjunction with the local show or village fete. They are very relaxed affairs and can prove a thoroughly enjoyable family outing, as well as a very gentle introduction to competitive showing.

Then there are dog matches, held by registered canine societies, where dogs compete in pairs, drawn at random, in a pyramid type system until at the end of the day there remains just one unbeaten dog. These, too, can be entered on the day. They can be great fun and also provide a vehicle for getting the new puppy or youngster used to mixing with other dogs and people, often in a relatively confined space. They also

The famous UK Ch. Maid For Gold at Armorique winning the Spillers/Dog World Puppy of the Year competition in 1994 for Shaune Frost & David Bates.

provide the opportunity to mix with other like-minded enthusiasts in the locality, and so can be popular social events.

The higher levels of shows need to be entered for in advance, on the entry form which will be found in the schedule of the appropriate show. Sanction shows and Limited Shows are open only to dogs which have not won a specified number of prizes. Sanction Shows, for example, are restricted to dogs which have not won five or more First Prizes at Open or Championship shows in Post Graduate classes and above. Both Sanction and Limited Shows are not open to any dogs which have won a

Challenge Certificate, or indeed any award that counts towards the title of Champion under the rules of any governing body recognised by the Kennel Club.

Sadly neither the Sanction or Limited Show are as numerous as in days gone by, as these were ideal training grounds for puppies and were invariably an afternoon or evening event judged by one judge, often a leading all-rounder. Many great dogs were "spotted" at such events and bought on the spot by judges who had an inherent eye for potential. Today the emphasis has shifted to the larger shows where Junior Warrant points and Challenge Certificates are on offer and seem to prove a temptation impossible to resist.

Basically Open shows are the same as Championship shows, but without Challenge Certificates available. The class definitions are the same and Champions are free to compete at Open shows. Due to the changing climate of dog shows, people these days seem far too keen to rush off to the Championship shows before they have really felt their feet at the smaller events, and regrettably the falling Open show entries bear testimony to that fact.

All the general shows are advertised in the weekly dog papers, as are many of the exemption shows nowadays.

THE BRITISH SHOW SYSTEM

A dog or bitch may only win the Kennel Club Challenge Certificate which counts towards the title of Champion at either a general or a Group Championship show or a breed club Championship show. Three certificates are needed, all awarded by different judges, before a

dog or bitch can be called a Champion and at least one must be won after the dog's first birthday.

The Kennel Club takes great care in allocating their Challenge Certificates to encourage and ensure the maximum competition, and so only one set of certificates is available to a breed on any one day anywhere in the British Isles. Particular care is also taken that there is a reasonable time lapse for exhibitors to travel between shows, especially during the busy summer months.

Since 1978 the number of Challenge Certificates awarded to a breed has been dependent on the total number of that breed exhibited at Championship shows, rather than as before, when a breed's annual registrations were the all-important factor.

Presently the certificate allocation is based on the actual numbers of exhibits at Championship shows, not entries made, taken as a one year's average over the previous three years, to which is added the average at breed club shows during the last of these years. The geographical spread and show dates are also taken into consideration when deciding the allocation, which is made two years in advance.

At the present time, Miniatures have certificates at twenty-three general shows and one Group Championship show and three breed Championship shows: the Miniature Club show is usually held at the beginning of October, the Schnauzer Club of Great Britain's usual date is March and the Northern Club usually hold their show at the beginning of November.

At Championship shows a reserve best of sex award is also made, if in the opinion of the judge the recipient is also an outstanding specimen; so should the certificate winner be disqualified for any reason, then the reserve may be awarded the certificate. Usually the Kennel Club contacts the judge in question for their opinion. No award challenge certificate or prize is automatically given and it may always be withheld.

In Britain, unlike at the AKC and FCI shows, the Champions and non-Champions compete against each other for the certificate, with the result that the emphasis in relation to a dog or bitch's show reputation generally rests on the number of these certificates and the number of bests of breed won, although more recently, since 1995 in fact, when the Group placings were extended to include the third and fourth placings, the Group placing has also taken on a new significance.

THE US SHOW SYSTEM
The AKC system of showing dogs is really quite different from that of other countries. To become a Champion, a dog must acquire 15 points. Part of the total must come in two "major" wins of 3, 4 or 5 points, under two different judges. The maximum a dog can win at one day's show is 5 points. Dogs competing for points do so in various classes, including puppy, novice, bred-by-exhibitor, American-bred and Open. All dogs and bitches competing for points are known as "class dogs". The winners of each dog class will compete

for "Winners Dog" and, with it, the award of the available points. After the male class dogs have been judged, the process is repeated for bitches, ending in a selection of "Winners Bitch". Champions of Record who are competing for Best of Breed are only judged after both the dog and bitch classes have been judged. Male and female Champions, called "Specials" compete with the Winners Dog and Winners Bitch. From this group, the judge will select Best of Breed, Best of Opposite Sex (to Best of Breed), and Best of Winners (from either Winners Dog or Winners Bitch). When a dog has accumulated the necessary fifteen points, it is said to have "finished."

The Best of Breed winner will go on to compete in the Group competition. At AKC shows, Group judges select first, second, third, and fourth placings. Obviously, only the first in Group goes on to compete with other Group winners for Best in Show.

Some Champions go on to be "specialled". Specialling a Champion means showing the dog regularly, generally in order to achieve a national ranking. A dog can achieve a ranked status by becoming the top winning dog in a region, defeating the same dogs over

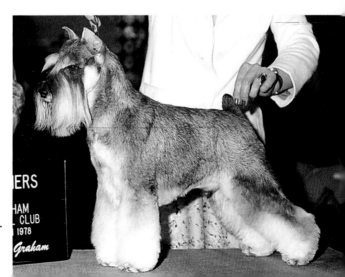

American Ch. Blythewood National Anthem (Am. Ch. Sky Rocket's Bound to Win ex Blythewood Symphony). Bred & owned by Mrs Joan Huber. Photo: Graham.

The ultimate for the American Schnauzer show enthusiast.

and over. Occasionally, a dog is campaigned. A campaigned dog will compete in different areas in the country, in the theory that a truly great dog should win anywhere, against all competitors. These dogs are the rare treasures.

There are no Championship shows as found in the United Kingdom. American dog shows are actually more comparable to the British Open shows, with total entries that range from 800 dogs to 2500 dogs. Often, local kennel clubs band together to hold a "cluster" of shows, covering three or four days of showing, all in the same location. In some areas there will be successive clusters within a few hundred miles of each other, and these are known as 'circuits.' The most famous circuit is the Florida circuit in January of each year, which draws enormous entries from the frozen snowbelt areas in the Northern United States, as well as many other locations.

THE FCI SYSTEM

With this system there are some variations and differences from country to country but, in the main, the following applies. The four colours are not only judged separately, but also enjoy separate Championship status. Under the FCI rules there are ten groups with all the three Schnauzer breeds being shown in Group Two, which includes such a diversity of breeds as the Dobermann, Affenpinscher, St. Bernard, Shar Pei, Boxer, Bulldog and Newfoundland, among others.

Breed classes have the sexes divided and are more limited than in Britain; all are age-related, except the Champions class. The winners of the puppy class, six to nine months, and youth class, nine to 18 months, may not win the National or International Certificate or be declared Best of Breed, but, if the judge feels any are of outstanding quality, then the honour prize may be given. This is greatly valued, and more than one may be awarded in these youth classes.

The Open class is for exhibits of fifteen months of age and over, while the Champions class is confined to title holders with a National or International Championship or both, recognised by the FCI. There is also a Veteran class for those of six years of age and over, but the winners may not compete for any Championships.

Although the national title requirements do vary slightly from country to country, in general a dog or bitch needs to win three certificates from at least two different judges, and with at least one year between the first and third certificates. Most also need one of the certificates to have been won at the

*Ch. USA, Int., Fran., Port. Sole Baye's
John Henry.
Bred by S. Phelps, owned by A. Pons.*

*Australian Ch. Wrendras Dream
Knight.
Bred by Mr & Mrs Ward in England.
Photo: Animal Pics.*

country's principal show – Brussels, Paris or Madrid, for example, or at a club show.

To become an International Champion, four international certificates are needed from at least three different judges and won in at least three different countries. Additionally, one of the certificates must also have been won in either the country the dog lives in or the country of origin for the breed – Germany in the case of all the Schnauzers.

Again there is the time factor of at least one year between the first and fourth certificates. The certificate may only be awarded from the open class upwards, and the recipient must be at least fifteen months of age. If a dog or bitch is already an International Champion, and therefore does not need the win, then the award goes to the reserve winner, but this is done later by the FCI in Brussels. The national and international certificates represent a high standard of excellence and are not automatically awarded. Interestingly, in most countries a Giant Schnauzer will also need to have won a working trial

certificate before it becomes a National or International Champion.

THE IRISH KENNEL CLUB SYSTEM

It is a points system for making Champions under the Irish system, which is dependent upon the number of dogs and bitches actually present and in competition at the show. The value of the Green Stars, as the points are called, can vary from year to year. They are reviewed annually and a green star index figure is worked out for each breed and sex and this then applies to all Championship shows scheduling the breed for the coming year.

This index figure is based on the previous year's entries of actual dogs and bitches shown in the breed at the recognised Championship shows. The highest value may be ten, and the lowest zero. If, for example, the index figure for males in a breed is five, then that number of males needs to be present and in competition for the five point green star to be awarded; if fewer dogs are present then the green star won only has the value of the number of dogs present. If there are more, then the value is

Irish Ch. Risepark Favorite Fella (Ch. Risepark Firm Favorite ex Ch. Sonshea Scarlett Streamers at Risepark). Bred by Peter Newman & Barry Day, owned by Paul Scanlon & Monica Betts. Top winning puppy, top Miniature, Pup of the Year and Dog of the Year qualifier. The first Irish Champion to become an English Champion. To date the most winning Miniature Schnauzer in Ireland.

increased. Likewise, if the green star index for bitches was eight, then eight bitches need to be present for a five point green star to be won; if fewer then the value is reduced, if more then it is increased.

Some shows have mixed sex classes and these have a different index value which is only won by the best of breed, and the value is usually a point higher than the breed's lower index figure.

Should the sex of the best of breed winner have the lower green star value, then that winner is automatically also allocated the higher points. This, it is felt, encourages healthy competition and also discourages any withdrawing to reduce the value of the green stars. Also, if a dog or bitch wins the Group, and any breed in that Group has a higher green star value than the Group winner,

then the Group winner will also automatically be given the higher green star value. Reserve green stars are also awarded and, if for any reason the green star winner is disqualified, then the reserve winner takes them, less one point for the disqualified dog.

A five point (or more) green star is called a major. To become an Irish Champion a dog or bitch needs a total of forty points, of which there must be at least four five-point green stars, with the remaining green stars being of any value to complete the total.

The Irish Kennel Club also make an annual award which is known as the Annual Champion. This is awarded to one dog in either sex of each breed, the recipient being the exhibit that has won the most points over 30 in the calendar year and that exhibit is then designated Annual Champion followed by the year of the award, e.g. Ch. Deansgate Well Fancied An. Ch. 1991.

GETTING STARTED

It is generally felt that the best way for a complete beginner to start is by entering at the smaller local shows. Special care should be taken when deciding where and when to introduce your latest hope to the experience of a dog show. It is always a good idea to take the puppy to a few show-training classes beforehand. Details of these can usually be obtained by contacting the Secretary of your local all-breeds club or canine society. They do prove a great help and provide valuable experience in giving to both the dog and the handler the basic ideas of just what lies ahead and what will be expected of them in the show ring. But do be sure that the classes for which you enrol are show-oriented ringcraft classes rather than Obedience classes. While you want your Miniature to be well-behaved and sociably acceptable, the need to "Sit" on command is not desirable in a show dog, and Obedience training can prove quite confusing.

The smaller shows are excellent for taking the initial plunge and gaining confidence, but remember they can often be quite crowded and cramped affairs, especially in the early part of the show. The whole idea is to have your dog and yourself enjoy the exercise, so be patient and unflustered. Give yourself plenty of time to get your dog ready for its class. We all feel nervous and self-conscious at times; just put these feelings to one side, relax and enjoy yourself. That is not to say that you should be flippant about the exercise and lose concentration when in the ring. Nothing can be more frustrating for a judge than finding a dog they really like being spoiled by an inattentive handler. Not all judges are renowned for their patience!

Summertime has the added advantage of some really lovely outdoor shows and venues. These are often held in conjunction with a town or agricultural show, and have all the extra attractions for the rest of the family that such shows can offer. These are splendid places to get the new entrants used to the idea, and into the ways, of showing. Often, too, the rings and conditions are less crowded and uncomfortable than are some of those to be found in indoor venues.

VARIETY CLASSES

It is always preferable to enter a show which has Miniature Schnauzers

Junior handling is now a popular activity worldwide - the international final of the junior handling competiton is held at Crufts each year.   *Photo: Jo Franklin.*

classified as a separate breed. However, the "Not Separately Classified" classes are also well worth considering and supporting if there are not separate classes for Miniatures. These classes are often generously scheduled and well graded, so that you will be able to enter appropriate classes within the scope of your dog and experience. Although the Not Separately Classified classes often present the strongest competition in the show, don't be put off – they are well worth entering and a win or placing will really mean something. Also, the chances are that these classes will be judged by the show's Best in Show judge. If this happens to be one of the really experienced All Rounders, you can be guaranteed a really knowledgeable opinion.

Sadly perhaps, the Variety classes are not as numerous nowadays as they used to be, but they still do provide interest and added competition. Remember that there can sometimes be quite long waits between classes, and in the judging of these classes, and this is especially so when most of the exhibits will not have been seen in a previous class by the Variety judge. A long wait can be tiring for a new entrant, especially if it is made to be on its best behaviour all the time. The over-riding factor should be to ensure that your Miniature Schnauzer really enjoys these all-important first outings.

SHOW TRAINING

Most dogs will have begun their training at any age from eight weeks onwards. They will have become used to being handled, to standing on the table to be examined, and being trimmed and groomed, as well as having their teeth and bite checked. They should, of course, become used to a show lead and to making the general movement patterns that will be expected of them in the show ring. They should be encouraged to pose freely and to become used to being set-up manually and handled on the ground. It is easier to build upon the natural friendliness and boldness of puppyhood if training is started young. Always remember that "a little at a time" is best with lessons. Never overtire or bore your puppy.

RING PROCEDURE

Most judges follow the same pattern as far as ring procedure goes. Before the individual examination, the exhibits are looked at collectively as they stand, lined-up in the ring. The dogs which are appearing for the first time in the particular class ("new" dogs, as opposed to "old" dogs which have been seen by the judge in an earlier and lower class) are then moved in a circle once or twice around the ring. This not only gives the dogs a chance to settle, but gives the judge and ringside an overall picture of the dogs in competition, and of the general quality and depth of the class. In the big, all-breed variety classes, there may not be room for this mass movement, in which case the judge will usually content himself with walking along the line of new exhibits as they stand, in order to gain an overall impression of quality and content.

Either way, it can be seen that there is value and importance in having your dog used to standing four-square, concentrating on his job, and freely showing off his good points for this most important first contact with the judge. Many judges have, more or less, made their mind up when they first see a class walk into the ring, certainly as to which dogs they are really interested in, so it behoves you to have your dog looking good and on his toes from the start. It is often a good idea, if you can, to collect your ring number before your class begins, when the ring steward is not too busy. Then, from the moment you first enter the ring, you will be able to concentrate wholly on getting the best out of your dog.

Miniature Schnauzers are mainly examined on the table. Some judges will ask the age, others not – so be prepared. All judges should examine the teeth and bite. Some judges prefer the exhibitors to show this themselves, others will make their own examination. After the individual table examination, where the judge will be handling the dog to ascertain construction, balance, coat texture etc., the exhibit will be required to move either straight up and down the ring, or in the form of a triangle, or both, so watch and listen to what is wanted. The triangle not only gives the straight up and down movement of the exhibit, but in profile it also gives the overall picture and balance. As well as showing the topline and set-on, the front reach and rear drive, it also shows how the exhibit uses itself in general on the move – in other words, its carriage. All this is being shown in one simple, straightforward uninterrupted movement.

At the end of this individual movement, the judge will invariably want to see your dog standing freely, still and looking alert. It may be that you will be asked to move again before this point, so be prepared and always listen carefully to any requests, since the judge may want your dog moved or shown in a different manner. If not, stop at a little distance from the judge at the end of your moving, and encourage your dog to show himself off, taking special care not to stand between your dog and the judge. At this point, most judges are particularly interested in re-checking the ear-set and expression, so it is as well to have your dog used to having his attention attracted to show off these particular points. This can be done when training, using either bait or some kind of favourite toy which can be guaranteed to get your dog to focus instantly. It will be seen that, bearing all this in mind, it is a good idea to watch what the other exhibitors have been doing in your class, or in any earlier classes the judge has judged at the show.

The puppy must get used to being set up.

Keep training sessions short, and your puppy will soon learn what is required.

A polished performance from an adult dog.

The handler must move his dog so that the judge can assess movement.

The dog must move with confidence.

The judge will usually wish to assess gait from the front, the rear and in profile.

When the individual examination and movement has been completed, the judge will thank you, or otherwise indicate that he has finished. Go to the side of the ring where the other dogs already seen will be lined up, and, if in doubt, ask the steward where you should stand with your dog.

TIPS FOR THE NOVICE
It can be a big help for the beginner to place himself in the middle or towards the end of the initial class line-up. However, in some countries, exhibitors are asked to stand in numerical order, although this does not normally happen in the UK. If you can get towards the end of the line, this gives you a little extra time to study the other exhibitors and see what is expected of you. Never be afraid to pause, or even start again, should your dog slip its lead (heaven forbid), shake, or otherwise misbehave. We all feel very self-conscious at such times, but do not let such things worry you; just try to collect yourself and your dog and carry on to put on a polished performance. Most judges are patient, especially with exhibitors who are obviously novices. A point worth remembering – sometimes, when the dogs are going around together, one of them may decide to be difficult and unco-operative. If this is yours, just step aside and let the other exhibitors pass by, then join on the end of the line when all is well. Doing this will save a great deal of embarrassment. It will not break the judge's concentration, nor cause any ill will amongst the other exhibitors.

With the individual examination of the dogs on the table, the next exhibitor can help things to flow by placing his dog as soon as the previous handler has left the table, so that when the judge has finished assessing one dog, the next is ready and waiting, nicely set up on the table. This is best done quietly when the previous dog is being gaited. Never put the other dog off, or move between it and the judge. One small but important point – when setting up your dog on the table, remember to have it facing the way the judge will want to see it when making his examination.

When you have joined the other dogs that have been seen, then is the time to re-straighten the beard and furnishings and generally tidy the exhibit by combing any stray hairs and cleaning up the outline. This has a steadying effect, and can give the opportunity for a few minutes breather while the remaining exhibits are being examined individually. You can relax a little here, and let your dog relax too, but do not let him do whatever he pleases and mess up his coat. It can be a good idea to stand between your dog and the judge at this point, to obstruct his view when relaxing your dog, particularly on a hot sunny day when you can provide some welcome shade. Do remember however that, firstly, some judges glance around the ring and assess and compare all the time, so it may be that your dog will have to forego this little breathing space, as it will be necessary to keep your dog on his toes throughout the class. Secondly, never get so engrossed in talking to the ringside or your neighbour that your dog goes completely slack and becomes inattentive, for you can be sure that this will happen just when your dog is noticed by the judge. You should make a point of studying the judge's

technique before your class (difficult, I know, if you are in the first class of the day) if possible, so that you are aware of his style of judging.

When the judge is examining his last "new" exhibit in the class, this is the time to check that your own dog is standing, looking well, and that the furnishings are all in place. Your dog should again now be looking and showing his very best. Most judges like to see their dogs standing, all facing the same way, and customarily dogs are shown with their heads facing to the handler's right, though if you happen to be left-handed, and feel more comfortable with your dog facing that way, few judges would insist on a reversal. Once he has seen the entire class, the judge may request that some of the exhibits in the class be moved again, or he may want to re-examine and check some points on individual dogs as they stand. Usually the judge will then pull out those he wishes to consider further, often in no particular order, dismissing the rest. Those remaining will often be handled and moved yet again, and then pulled out in the order of the final placings. Wherever you are placed, there is still the need to concentrate and keep your dog showing and looking good. Never give up, since there is often that final pause and look before the judging book is marked. Right up to the last moment, the placings can be changed.

MISTAKES TO AVOID
One mistake which is often made by the experienced handler as much as by the rank novice is interfering and overfussing with their dog. Remember that if the judge asks you to show or position your

exhibit in a certain way, do it and leave it alone. The judge is trying to help you; it is what he wants, and he is the one who matters on the day. This does illustrate the need to have your dog not only used to showing freely but, also, to being "stacked" if necessary, that is being easily and gently held in position, with the show lead reasonably tight and held high up the neck, and the tail held in position by placing one or two fingers behind it. It is also in this stance that the dog is best presented when being individually examined on the table. It is a great mistake to "string up", in other words, to hold the lead so tight and the dog so rigid that it looks completely unnatural and uncomfortable.

There is a tendency for some people to prepare their dogs at a show far too early for their class. When the time comes for the dog to go into the show ring it is bored and fed up, and does not give of its best, as it will have been standing on its grooming table for hours. It is far better to leave the dog on its bench, or in its crate, resting and relaxed for as long as possible. Only start the final grooming with enough time to do so in comfort and without rushing. Also, make sure that your dog has had enough time to relieve himself and loosen up before going into the ring. In this way he will not feel overfussed or fed up, but be fresh, comfortable and raring to go into the ring and do himself, and you, justice by rewarding all the hard work and effort that you have put into his preparation.

Just as a suggestion, it is a good idea to have a show cage or crate which your dog can get used to long before his first show. Many shows are crowded or unbenched and this facility does mean that your exhibit can rest in complete security and comfort out of the draughts, and undisturbed by people and other dogs. A show cage or crate will leave you free to move about with an easy mind. It will also eliminate the need for you to leave your dog in the car on a hot day. Needless to say, having your own grooming table at the show makes good sense and takes away all the hassle that would occur without one.

BREED CLUB SHOWS
Breed Club shows are really in a class of their own. They prove great fun and are most enjoyable. Generally they draw much bigger entries than the all-breeds shows, so you can see a much wider cross-section of the breed. They have an attractive classification, with much more choice of classes – especially for a newer owner and exhibit – and breed shows tend to be more relaxed and informal affairs, rather akin to a family gathering. You will find at the breed shows, more than at the bigger shows, that people have more time to mix and socialise, and to get to know each other. The experienced breeders will be less frantic, and when they have free time will generally be perfectly happy to help and advise on all aspects of Miniature Schnauzer ownership and competition. Most breeders have the good of the breed at heart, and derive great joy from seeing a top-class specimen well presented and handled – regardless of ownership – and some may well, quite uninvited, offer a few words of advice regarding your handling or coat presentation. If this happens, do not take offence, but be grateful for their

thoughtfulness and heed their words.

Should you be seeking help, do pick your moment. Often breeders are approached just when they are arriving or settling their dogs in at the show, or when they are preparing their own dogs. No one likes to be bothered at such times, and you might run the risk of being at the receiving end of a very rough tongue from someone who, under different circumstances, would have been only too happy to spend time with you. So be warned. Breeders and exhibitors are not as uninterested or off-hand as they may at first appear. Most would agree that, however confident, established or experienced exhibitors they are, everyone gets just that little bit tense before going into the ring – rather like actors waiting in the wings. What may surprise some people is that, after a class is over, some exhibitors are almost totally unaware of the other exhibitors and exhibits that were in the class or what they had done, so engrossed were they in their own exhibit.

SHOWING IN PERSPECTIVE
Showing can be a very rewarding hobby if it is seen in perspective and it is realised that it is not life and death. You can become involved in showing your Miniature Schnauzer whatever level you choose, from attending the occasional Exemption show through the summer, to hard campaigning at all the Championship shows if you have a really top-class dog which is a potential winner. The secret is to look at your dog quite objectively and establish in your mind its level of quality and merit. Then show accordingly. It is pointless taking a poor-quality dog to show after show when it will be up against far superior specimens. Many people first venture into the show ring with their initial dog, bought purely as a companion. They then realise that this dog may well not quite be exhibition quality, so then they specifically look for a show dog.

There is a well-known saying that should never be forgotten: win or lose, always remember that the dog you are taking home with you at the end of the show is exactly the same dog you brought with you that morning.

6 THE COLOURS

While pepper and salt, black, and black and silver are the most popular colours of Miniature Schnauzer, and the only colours acceptable by the Kennel Club and American Kennel Club's Breed Standards, white is now an acceptable colour under the FCI Standard adopted in 1995. Furthermore, due to their somewhat chequered ancestry, occasionally puppies of other coat colours and patterns are born to litters of Miniature Schnauzers, among them black and tan and particolour.

BLACK AND SILVERS

For many years the breed in Britain was basically either black, or pepper and salt, as far as the show ring was concerned and the pioneer breeders worked solely with these colours. However, interest in the less popular black and silver has grown steadily over the years, and when the Kennel Club revised all the Breed Standards in 1985, they accepted black and silver as a third colour in Miniatures.

Since then, dogs and bitches bred by Eastwight, Rownhams, Arbeybuffels, Ripplevale, Viento and Proscenium have proved to be the main influence on the breeding of this colour in Britain. Furthermore, the top winning black and silvers, American Ch. Feldmar Night Reveler and, later, American Ch. Feldmar Pistol Pete, en route to Mike Brick of the Brickmark Miniature Schnauzers in New Zealand, did their quarantine and fulfilled their residency requirements in Britain. Before completing the final leg of their journey, they were exclusively used by Ted and Sally Ilott and, as a result, their Leecurt black and silvers carry this Feldmar blood in their back pedigrees.

BLACK AND SILVER CHAMPIONS

The first black and silver Champion was Pam and Dave Wicks' Ch. Qassaba Tia Christel who finished in 1986 at the Miniature Club's Championship show under Elaine Quigley. She was also the first black and silver to qualify for a Junior Warrant. Her first Certificate was won, with Best of Breed, at the Welsh Kennel Club earlier in the year under the late Robert M. James, one of Britain's

Ch. Ashwick The Real McCoy (Proscenium Bilbo Baggins ex Ch. Quassaba Tia Christel).
Owned by Miss M. Price. Bred by Mr & Mrs D.T. Wick
The first English black & silver dog Champion, finished in 1991.

Rownhams Impressario (Eastwight Sea Encounter ex Rownhams Concerto). Bred and owned by Mrs E. Quigley. The first black & silver to win a Challenge Certificate in England, and an influential sire of this colour.
Photo: Anne Roslin-Williams.

Sea-Conflict of Eastwight.
Owned by Miss P. Morrison-Bell.
A Challenge Certificate winning black & silver, born in 1983, who is behind many of the more recent winning black & silvers.
Photo: Anne Roslin-Williams.

Ch. Eastwight Sea-Mannikin.
Bred & owned by Miss P. Morrison-Bell. The first black & silver Champion for his breeder, made up in 1993.
Photo: Diane Pearce.

Leecurt Silver Lace. Bred and owned by Mr & Mrs T. Ilott. A typical Leecurt black & silver. Photo: Sally Anne Thompson.

Ch. Sedir Davy Crocket.

busiest and best-respected all-rounder judges. The second came at Richmond under specialist judge Betty Fletcher, and again with it Best of Breed. A further win at the Utility Breeds show under Archie Fletcher secured for Tia Christel the position of top winning Miniature bitch of that year.

It was not until 1991 that the colour had its first male Champion and this was Marilyn Price's Ch. Ashwick The Real McCoy when he won his third CC and Best of Breed) under Betty Fletcher at WELKS. Bred by the Wicks, he is out of Ch. Qassaba Tia Christel and sired by Proscenium Bilbo Baggins, another who traces back to Eastwight Sea Wizard. His other Certificates were won in 1989 at Darlington under Knut-Sigurd Wilberg and the following year under Archie Fletcher at Three Counties.

Carol and Terry Parnell's Ch. Minivale Georgie Girl was the second black and silver bitch to finish and that was in 1995. Sired by Ch. Arbey Ard T' Match,

she was the second Champion for her dam, Minivale Talk of the Town, who carries Ch. Ashwick The Real McCoy, Ch. Arbey Archer, Ch. Qassaba Tia Christel and the imported Suelen Rum Punch at Arbey and Buffels in her immediate background.

The first Junior Warrant winning black and silver male was Rosemary Wallace's Viento Silver Slippers (Silver Socks of Rownhams ex Ripplevale Frosty Jabot) who won the final points at the Schnauzer Club's Open show in 1987. A good Stakes win enjoyed by the colour was back in 1983 when Pam Morrison-Bell's Eastwight Sea Conflict won the Junior Stakes at South Wales under Douglas Appleton.

Although appreciated by Schnauzer specialists, the black and silvers do not seem as yet to enjoy the same recognition among all-breed judge as the pepper and salts and blacks, but that could all change as the breed develops and more become attracted to this attractive colour, with increasing numbers in the show ring.

BLACK MINIATURES
Somehow, interest in the blacks over the years has always been somewhat limited and spasmodic. Mrs Boubelik, a pre-war enthusiast, was to continue active after the war when she imported from Austria the black dog, Dyk v. Robertshof, to blend with her Oldstock blacks. Despite the further efforts of Mrs Reynolds, Wally Butterfield, Phyl and Fred Morley and, latterly, Gill Barwick, Pat Bretherton, Jo and Brian Braybrooke and Val Sutcliffe, as well as encouragement through restricted colour classes at the breed shows, the blacks have never become anywhere near as well-established or popular in post-war years in Britain as the pepper-and-salts. Certainly they are nothing like as numerous as they are in Europe and also more recently the USA. However, it is pleasing to see that interest here in Britain has at last begun to grow quite noticeably from the early 1990s.

The influence of several black American-bred Skansen imports, blended with dogs of Ripplevale, Rillaton, Bryher, Nixador and Jenmil, along with others of British backgrounds, has been effective in giving the black Miniatures a style, sturdiness and type that had been lacking in so many of the colour hitherto. The Saleisma, Sybray and Chloella breeding are also all playing an important part in the development of the present-day blacks.

BLACK CHAMPIONS
The first post-war black Champion was

Mrs Jo Reynolds' Italian-bred Ch. Jovinus Malya Swanee, bred by Mrs Pozzi. He finished in 1963 and was also Best in Show at the Miniature Club's Championship show that year, under the author – the second club show success enjoyed by Mrs Reynolds with a black. The first had been two years previously, when Jovinus Risotto went Best in Show under Schnauzer specialist Mrs Board. Risotto, when mated to Swanee, produced the first post-war British-bred black Champion, Jovinus Replica, who finished in 1969.

Barway Bitter Lemon and Burnt Toast, two daughters of Ch. Jovinus Malya Swanee bred by Wally Butterfield, proved particularly interesting as blacks. Bitter Lemon was the first Miniature of Fred and Phyl Morley (Castilla), and won the Bitch CC at Richmond in 1964 under Schnauzer specialist Glyn Bright. Burnt Toast, when mated to the pepper-and-salt Risepark Northern Cockade, produced the black dog Barway Bartender, the best of this colour Wally Butterfield felt he had ever bred. Sold as a pet as a young puppy, Bartender, as a result, only had a limited show and stud career.

Mrs Barwick made several black importations. The first, Basirious Xeros, came from Sweden in 1975. He had van Stedeke, the breeding of the Countess de Pret, and del Tornese blood in his pedigree. Next, from Mrs Eskrigge in the USA, came the bitch, Yavaleska Anfiger who whelped a litter to US Ch. Kelly's Black Onyx in quarantine. From this a dog, Black Yankee of Ripplevale, was campaigned by Mrs Barwick against the pepper-and-salts with some success. His brother, Black Yavaleska of

Ch. Jovinus Malya Swanee.
Bred in Italy by Mrs Pozzi, owned by Mrs Reynolds.
The first post-war black champion in England, finished in 1964.

Chloella Bon Ton at Sybray
Owned by Mr & Mrs Braybrooke
The Crufts Challenge Certificate winner 1988.

Photo: Bull.

Ch. Saleima Imperial Black at Sybray (Saleima Black Knight ex Saleima Black Opel). Bred by Mrs Bretherton, owned by Mr & Mrs B. Braybrooke.
The second post-war English black bitch Champion to date, finished in 1989.

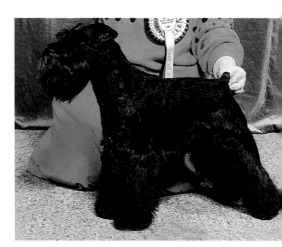

Ch. Black Bijou at Jenmil (Rillaton Black Moonman ex Time for Reflection).
Bred by Mrs Carveley, owned and shown by Mrs Milburn.
The second post-war black male Champion, finished in 1992.

Ch. World, Euro, Int., Esp., Fran., Port., Mon. Rayma Faria.
Bred by Cristobal Ramus, owned by A. Pons.

*Ch. World 92, Int., Esp.
Port. Nocko v Havenstad.
Bred by C. du Meulenaer,
owned by C. Ramos.*

Ripplevale, was also retained. Later, also from the USA, came the bitch, Kelly's Ebony of Ripplevale, carrying Kelly's, Jo-Mar's and Gough's bloodlines. She was mated to Black Yavaleska and from this mating Ripplevale Black Ivan was retained. This youngster came in for some favourable comments when he won Puppy Dog at the Schnauzer Club Show of 1982, but was never extensively campaigned.

At the Northern Schnauzer Club's 1987 Championship show, judged by Herr Höller, the President of the Pinscher-Schnauzer Klub in Germany, awarded the Reserve CC to Joan and Brian Braybrooke's black bitch, Chloella Bon Ton at Sybray, a daughter of Sybray Black Bounty Hunter and Ebony Charm at Chloella and bred by Val Sutcliffe. At that time, this was the highest win achieved by a black for something like twenty years. At the following Crufts she won the Bitch CC under Elaine Quigley, also qualifying for her Junior Warrant, the first of her colour to do so. Val Sutcliffe retained her littermate, the male Chloella Black Magic, who won the Minor Puppy Stakes at Leicester under Cyril Williams and was then declared Best Puppy Dog – another high point

for the blacks. In 1987 the Braybrookes also won the Reserve CC with their home-bred black-and-silver, Sybray Frosty Candy Kisses (Proscenium Bilbo Baggins ex Ripplevale Frosty Kiss 'n' Hug) at Birmingham City under Maurice Marshall.

History was written on behalf of the blacks at the Miniature Club's 1989 Championship show, when the judge Fred Morley awarded both CCs to exhibits of this colour. The male was Val Sutcliffe's home-bred Chloella Black Rod (Chloella Black Magic ex Chloella Silver Serenade), who won Best of Breed and also Best Puppy, while the Braybrookes' Saleima Imperial Black at Sybray (Saleima Black Knight ex Saleima Black Opal) won the Bitch CC. She was bred by Pat Bretherton. These two were to repeat their success shortly afterwards at the British Utility Breeds show under Pam McLaren, but this time the bitch went Best of Breed and with this third CC became a Champion, the first black title-holder since the sixties and only the third of the colour in total. At the show her class win also gave her the final points for her Junior Warrant.

It was also at the Utility Breeds show, in 1992, that Jennifer Milburn's Ch.

Sybray Snow Crystal. A white bitch, bred and owned by Mr & Mrs Braybrooke.

Black Bijou at Jenmil won his third CC to give him his title, making him the first British-bred black male Champion. During his career he also won twelve Reserve CCs and was also the top sire of 1995 through the successes of his two black Jenmil puppies out of Bryher Black Busy Lizzie – Black Quartz and Black Crystal. Another special win for Mrs Milburn was at the earlier Utility Breeds show in 1989 when the pepper and salt, Jenmil Master Matelot, went Best Puppy in Show.

Bijou has an interesting background in that he is black-bred paternally and pepper and salt bred on his maternal side. On his sire's side he traces to the imported Skansens Moonracer to Zantana, a son of Am. Ch. Regency's Shot In The Dark, and also to Walters Champions, while his dam's pedigree carries Iccabod, Castilla, Beaulea and Vandell lines.

The latest black to make an impact is Caroline and Steve Wareing's male, Skansens Toyboy at Caskayd, a son of Am. Ch. Skansens Toys R Us and Skansens Quizas. The Best Puppy in Show at the Northern Club show on his debut, and then won the CC at the Utility Breeds' silver jubilee show, his next outing. He brought the colour to great prominence by winning Best of Breed at Crufts in 1997.

WHITE MINIATURES

While white Miniatures are still not embraced by the Breed Standard of either the Kennel Club or the AKC, it is a recognised colour under FCI rules. This attractive colour seems to have first begun appearing in numbers in the early fifties, although there is evidence going back to the thirties and forties that occasional white puppies were born in litters of predominantly black and pepper and salt litters. At that time, however, they were not bred from or encouraged. In Anne Paramoure's book *The Complete Miniature Schnauzer* appears a photograph of a single litter containing three white puppies, two pepper and salts and one black and silver.

In the late forties and early fifties, in Germany, whites were occurring in litters from black-to-black matings, and the Pinscher Schnauzer Klub came under strong pressure to recognise the colour. As a result, a few breeders were given special dispensation to mix colour matings, but only allowing white to black, to allow a gene pool to build up. In the early seventies, when it was considered that a sufficient number of whites had been produced in this way, and a sensible-sized gene pool created, the dispensation ceased and breeders were only then permitted to mate white to white. Although the colour has never grown in popularity to the same extent as the black and silver, whites are nevertheless being actively bred in Germany, Poland, the Czech Republic and Russia, as well as in smaller numbers in some other European countries.

Under the Fédération Cynologique Internationale rules, the white Miniatures are now allowed to be shown and have Championship status in their own right in most European countries, but their entries are, of course, nothing like as large as the other colours.

A litter containing black, black & silver and white puppies, bred by Mrs Anne Scott of the Busco kennels.

GENETIC MAKE-UP

The white colour appeals to some, but it should not be thought of as an albino. According to Mrs Paramoure "No albinos had been recorded in the breed in any country up to 1950."

Genetically the white colour is recessive and therefore is similar to the black and silver gene, which is also recessive. Black is dominant, which means that any colour, including the pepper and salts, would be able to carry the white gene, and, providing both parents carried it (regardless of what their physical colour was), it would be possible to produce whites.

So far, in Britain, the number of whites is very small and they have come about through line-breeding. They first appeared around the end of the eighties from a mating between black and silvers having a predominantly continental background.

In 1993 when Brian and Joan Braybrooke twice mated their black, Ch. Saleima Imperial Black of Sybray to the black, Saleima Black Sirius, she produced two whites in each litter. One of these, Sybray Snow Crystal, was the first of the colour to be shown in the UK. This was at the Northern Club's Championship show, where she was placed fourth in a strong puppy bitch class by Miss Pamela McLaren.

When these puppies were born, they were white (not in any way greyish) and had pink points and noses which only after seven to ten days turned black. When the eyes opened, they were very dark with black rims around the eyelids, and the nails were also dark. Having this dark pigment and eyes was extremely pleasing, as good pigment is highly desirable with the white colour.

THE PARTICOLOUR

The particolour is basically a white ground colour with black and/or pepper and salt patches or markings, and it occurred in the breed in its early years, possibly coming through the use of the harlequin Miniature Pinscher in the breed's formative years. In Britain they have appeared just once, as far as is known, and that was in the late fifties from a mating of two pepper and salts. The resulting puppies were all sold as pets and never bred from. The mating was never repeated.

7 MATING, WHELPING AND WEANING

If your interest in the Miniature Schnauzer breed has deepened beyond just taking your dog to shows, there is every possibility that you may decide to become involved with breeding at some level.

Possibly your first dog is a male who has been successful in the show ring and admired by other breeders and exhibitors, in which case you may be approached to use him at stud. There is a popular misconception that a stud dog is merely a male of the breed with two testicles, but nothing could be further from the truth. A "stud dog" should be a male whose type, conformation and breeding suggest that he has something positive to offer the breed and, unless

Ch. Malenda Master Blend at Risepark. Bred by Mrs G. Allen, owned by Messrs Newman & Day. A superb showman and influential sire.

Photo: Sally Anne Thompson.

your Miniature is such a dog, it would be folly to allow him to sample pleasures which he has happily done without. If, however, you have been assured by experienced breeders that your dog has something to offer the breed, then there is no reason why he should not placed at stud to suitable bitches.

CARING FOR THE STUD DOG

First and foremost the stud dog should have a normal, happy and companionable life no different from that of any other dog. If he is allowed to mix freely with other dogs, studs are perfectly normal and balanced and should never become aggressive or difficult. Dogs are pack animals and their natural instinct and nature is towards companionship; keeping a stud dog in splendid isolation is asking for a difficult, aggressive and unmanageable animal.

It is important that the stud dog should not only be kept fit and healthy, but he should be fed correctly and well exercised. He should not be allowed to become over-fat and should be provided with good conditions in housing and general care.

It is usually advisable to use a dog for the first time when he is around a year old, though dogs will vary as individuals and some may express an interest in bitches at a considerably younger age than others. The number of times he is used, or his age, are not really factors which will affect his efficiency or attitude, but rather the way in which he effects his matings. A dog will quickly tire and become a troublesome stud, turn difficult about eating and become thoroughly upset and fractious, if he chases around for an hour or so and is

Hideki Checkpoint Charlie Risepark (English/Irish Champion Risepark Here Comes Charlie ex Penlan Pleased to Meet You).
Bred by Mr & Mrs McDonald, owned by Peter Newman & Barry Day.
An exciting combination of the American Irrenhaus and Penlan lines.
Photo: Jo Franklin

ultimately unsuccessful in mating a bitch, and again unsuccessful when he is tried later in the day, and maybe at other times too. This will take more out of him mentally and physically than several straightforward matings. Much can be done, with a little care and forethought, to help a stud and to make for an easy, straightforward mating and prevent any possible problems.

SENSIBLE MATING

Sometimes even the most experienced of

Am. Ch. Skylines Blue Spruce: Sire of 55 American Champions.

Photo: Mikron.

stud dogs will not be willing to mate a bitch, even though she appears ready and it is felt to be the right day for her. Do take notice of this. Your dog – and nature – knows best, and it is better to leave the mating for a day or so, until the stud dog is really keen to mate the bitch without any persuasion. The bitch is far more likely to conceive from such a mating than if you have forced a mating on the day you felt to be the right one.

If you are mating a maiden bitch, it is usually advisable to test that her passage is clear and to ensure that there is no stricture by greasing the little finger and gently inserting it to stretch her. This

can also make the mating easier for both the dog and the bitch. Do make sure that your hands are thoroughly clean before doing this, and for hygiene's sake, wearing a thin sterile plastic glove is advisable.

Neither the dog nor the bitch should ever be hurt or frightened at a mating, otherwise a stud may become shy, unsure of himself and unwilling to deal with a difficult bitch. No tension, shouting or striking either dog should ever occur at a mating; the atmosphere should be one of calm reassurance, and both the dog and bitch should be constantly encouraged and never curbed.

ASSISTING AT THE MATING
If you are allowing your dog to be used for the first time, it is to be recommended that you should invite an experienced breeder, who is familiar with stud work, to assist and advise. If the bitch's owner is such a person, then no further intervention will be necessary.

Initially the dog and the bitch should be allowed to play and become acquainted. The bitch should be kept on a lead and gently controlled if she is reluctant and difficult. If she is in any way aggressive, her muzzle should be tied, but not too tightly, with a soft bandage. The couple should be allowed five minutes or so of flirting, as this foreplay is an important part of the mating process.

When the dog appears ready to mount the bitch, she should be firmly held in position and kept steady. It is easier if two people are available to help with the mating, as one can steady the bitch by holding her collar and supporting her front, so that she cannot turn around

Ch. Risepark Chase the Ribbons (American-bred Ch. Irrenhaus Impact at Risepark ex Iccabod Daydreamer at Risepark).
Bred & owned by Peter Newman & Barry Day.
The 10th Champion for her sire.
Photo: Sally Anne Thompson.

Ch. Iccabod Mixed Herbs (Ch. Iccabod Chervil ex American bred Champion Travelmors From US to You).
Bred By Miss Radford & Mrs Clarke, owned by Mr & Mrs Clark.
One of the breed's top sires.
Photo: Sally Anne Thompson.

sharply at the moment of penetration, while the other can support the bitch's rear if necessary – some bitches may attempt to sit down – while the stud's owner can then concentrate on controlling the stud.

It can be helpful to provide a firm wooden platform about one inch or so deep and about eighteen inches square, or a non-slip mat of similar proportions. This should be placed behind the bitch to enable the stud to be at an easy height and have a firm, non-slip foundation which will give him good grip when he begins to work himself into the bitch. This is especially helpful when the bitch is a little taller than the dog, and will compensate for any height difference, while standing the bitch on such a base will help when the position is reversed. Obviously no two matings are the same, and oftentimes trial and error is necessary before you get the dog and bitch at the optimum levels.

THE TIE
There is knack in helping the stud at the actual time of entry which can soon be mastered. When the stud actually makes contact, he can be assisted and supported by having a helping hand placed on his bottom which can aid the thrusting process until the dog has fully penetrated the bitch and the "tie" is effected. The dog should be supported on top of the bitch for a minute or so after he has obviously tied. He can then either be left in that position or "turned", by lifting one of his hind legs over the bitch so that the dog and bitch are effectively standing back-to-back. Care should be taken when turning, so as not to hurt either dog or bitch, and they will then stand happily in the back-to-back position (which is quite natural – in the wild this position was adopted to avoid attack) until the tie subsides. This can be anything from five to fifty minutes!

Sometimes the bitch will want to pull

away or turn, so care should be taken to hold them together quite firmly but gently, until such time as they can part with ease. Invariably the stud dog will want to nuzzle his bitch after mating and whisper sweet nothings in her ear. Do not discourage this, as it is all part of the mating ritual.

Some dogs do not tie easily, and will swell up outside the bitch. If this is the case, the dog should be held in position until the ejaculatory process is complete. A tie is not always necessary to get a bitch in whelp. A mating where a tie is not effected is often referred to as a "slip mating".

PROBLEM MATINGS

If a stud is reluctant to mount a bitch, he can be teased and encouraged by gently moving the bitch around and lifting her rear end towards and away from him. When he does try to mount, encourage him. He should never be discouraged. Once he is firm and in the mood, he can soon be encouraged and directed to mount the correct end.

If, for some reason, a stud dog gets over-excited and ejaculates before a mating has been effected, he should be put away and left quietly for at least an hour before trying again. There is much misunderstanding where stud dogs are concerned, and some stud dog owners are reluctant to allow their dogs to be used too frequently. In reality, a young, healthy, fertile stud dog can successfully impregnate several bitches on the same day.

AFTER THE MATING

When the mating has been accomplished, the dog and the bitch should be left quietly for a while. Check that your stud dog's penis has gone back into its sheath, as sometimes there can be an "air bubble" which prevents full retraction. This can be removed manually by gently holding the base of the penis and slowly pulling towards the end. It is advisable to wash the dog's genitals with a mild antiseptic solution before returning him to his kennel-mates.

STUD DOG TERMS

If you have a dog at stud, be sure to explain the terms of service to the owner of the bitch. Normally the stud fee is payable at the time of service, after which you should give to the bitch's owner the appropriate Kennel Club form, verifying the mating and signed by the owner of the stud dog. The stud fee is for the service, and not any resulting puppies, though it is normally considered good practice to offer a free return service, should the bitch miss. However, this is a courtesy and not a right. Taking a puppy in lieu of a stud fee can be hazardous and has been known to end many a friendship. Far better to simply take your stud fee. If, when you see the litter, you fancy a puppy which is available, you can always negotiate with the breeder.

THE BROOD BITCH

If your venture into breeding involves taking a litter from your bitch, you should be confident that – as with the stud dog – she is an individual who has something to offer the breed. She should be typical, sound in construction and temperamentally stable. It is an added bonus if she herself has been bred from proven producing lines.

Having established that your bitch is suitable for mating, finding the best available stud dog for her is of paramount importance and a decision which requires much thought and research. There are fundamentally three types of breeding – outcrossing (where the dog and bitch have no common ancestors for at least five generations), line-breeding (where there are common ancestors in both pedigrees) and in-breeding (where the dog and bitch are very closely related, e.g. brother and sister, grandsire and grand-daughter).

Generally speaking, if you are intent on establishing a successful kennel you would be best advised to opt for one of the two latter alternatives. Outcrossing may well produce the odd quality puppy, but the litter will generally lack uniformity and be quite varied. In-breeding should only be undertaken by the most experienced, or with the benefit of advice from such people, who know intimately all the dogs in the relevant pedigrees along with their virtues and faults.

LINE-BREEDING
The most sensible course to follow will probably be line-breeding, and to do this successfully you need to examine your bitch's pedigree closely and evaluate the most successful dogs which appear in it at least once. If, for example, your bitch is a grand-daughter of a famous Champion dog whose photographs you have admired, you could be looking to find a son, or a grandson, of the same dog who excels in any points where your bitch may be lacking. Let us suppose that your bitch has a slightly light eye;

you should investigate the grandsire to which you are proposing to line-breed and establish that the light eye did not come from him. There is a 75 per cent chance that she inherited the eye colour from one of her other grandparents. If her grandsire had good eye colour, then find a descendant male who himself has excellent eye colour and who complements your bitch in general stamp and make-up. This could be an ideal choice. Do not rush off to use the latest Champion just because of his winning record. He may not suit your bitch either in breeding or in type.

HEALTH CHECKS
Your brood bitch should be typical with no really outstanding faults or hereditary problems. The main cause for concern within the breed, as far as such conditions go, relate to eyes, as cases of both Congenital Cataract and Progressive Retinal Atrophy have been found in Miniature Schnauzers in Britain. It is therefore important to buy from breeders who have had their stock checked, and, before breeding a litter, ensure that both stud dog and brood bitch have been checked. Testing sessions are regularly held by the breed clubs and further information is easily obtained from any club secretary.

Cataracts (both hereditary and congenital forms) and Generalised Progressive Retinal Atrophy (GPRA) occur in the Miniature Schnauzer. Every endeavour must be made to eradicate such problems from the breed, and it is strongly recommended that all Miniature Schnauzers are eye-tested annually by vets registered to perform such eye examinations.

Puppies can be eye-tested for the Congenital Hereditary form of Cataract at about six to eight weeks of age, before their sale as show dogs or pets. Identification of either Hereditary Cataract (HC) or PRA requires annual examinations, as these conditions both develop later. HC can only be diagnosed from about six months onwards and, sometimes, even later than two years of age. PRA may not appear until three years of age upwards, but may be detected in some breeds at any point between six months and six years. The earliest reported case in Miniature Schnauzers was in a three-year-old dog.

It is therefore imperative that all Miniature Schnauzers, especially breeding stock, are checked up to about eight years of age. Ask your breeder or vet to give you more information. If your dog is diagnosed with any of these problems, it is in the interest of all Miniature Schnauzers to advise the Miniature Schnauzer Club (via the Secretary) and the breeder.

Difficulties can occur even in the most carefully planned breeding programmes, but it is only through this exchange of information that we will eventually eradicate these problems from our favourite breed. It is important that the owners of the sire and dam know, because neither dog nor bitch should be bred from again. Also, it is important to let owners of the other puppies in the litter know, because these should not be bred from either.

Because of the mode of inheritance – recessive – it is not possible to identify those dogs which carry the gene. This can only be shown up by a test-mating programme, or by owners of affected dogs advising other owners, through their national Miniature Schnauzer Club, so that alternative action can be taken for the future. Researchers are working on a blood test to identify the defective gene which causes PRA but there is still a tremendous amount of work to do.

In the UK the Miniature Schnauzer Club, in conjunction with other breed clubs, supports the BVA/KC Eye Testing Scheme, organises eye-testing sessions and gives financial support to the PRA research programme. The club is also making strong representations to the BVA/KC co-ordinators to ensure that the cost of eye examinations is kept to the lowest possible levels.

THE BITCH'S CONDITION

Your bitch should be sound and typical, and although she should have a good roomy body, spacious heart and lung room, and a good depth of ribbing, she should still be feminine: there is no reason for her to be coarse in any way. Above all, she should be solid in temperament and have an inherent look of quality. It is better to have one minor fault in an otherwise good bitch, than to have a mediocre one with no particular virtues or good points, even though she may have no grave shortcomings. It is easier to breed out one fault than it is to try to breed in several virtues.

When she is mated, the bitch should be in good hard condition and not over-fat. It is also a good idea to have her stool checked to see if she is free of worms, and it can be advisable, at the start of her season, to have her swabbed and tested for any infection; if any is present a course of antibiotics will probably be recommended.

THE BITCH IN SEASON

Most bitches come into season for the first time between six and nine months. Thereafter they generally come into season at approximately six-monthly intervals. The length of the season varies from about 18 to 21 days. The first indication is a swelling of the vulva and bleeding (usually referred to as "showing colour"). This will persist for around 10 days, after which the colour will change from the bright red to pink and then a straw-like shade. This is usually when the bitch will be most receptive to the dog. It is the odour of the urine of the in-season bitch that attracts the male. Remember not to use any type of anti-mating preparation during the season if you intend mating your bitch. All types, whether spray or tablet, reduce the in-season scent of the bitch. It is this which attracts and stimulates the dog. He will not mate her if this is absent. It cannot be stressed how important it is that a bitch is securely confined during her season, especially during the latter period.

It is generally felt that the third season, when the bitch is at least eighteen months old, is the earliest age at which she should be mated. Most bitches are ready for mating between the 11th and the 14th day from the start of the season, but it is not at all easy to be sure exactly when the bitch begins her season, and recent advances in the understanding of the bitch's reproductive cycle suggest that ovulation varies from bitch to bitch. Some will be ready as soon as they are ready to stand for the dog; others will be ready later, even though they will have been happy to stand for several days. Counting days is not the best way to determine the optimum day of mating; it is far better to see how the bitch reacts. If you do not have the stud dog on your property, a good way of checking is to simply scratch the bitch's back near the root of her tail. If she is ready, she will twitch her tail from side to side, arch her back and lift her vulva, indicating that she is ready for mating over the next day or so. The experienced stud dog will investigate and make his own decision; a knowledgeable stud will ignore a bitch until the moment is right.

THE PREGNANT BITCH

The actual mating process has been covered earlier in this chapter when discussing the stud dog. Once your bitch has been mated, take her home and hope. Do not change her diet or routine in any way until at least six weeks after mating.

The period of gestation runs from 58 to 63 days, the average being 63 days, or nine weeks. Puppies can survive if they are born between the 53rd and 71st day; they are less likely to survive the more premature they are.

The diet of an in-whelp bitch is of great importance, for it must be of sufficient quality and quantity to sustain herself and bring about the development of her family in embryo. Therefore, it should contain vitamins, carbohydrates, fats, proteins and minerals. Egg yolks should be added to milk and cereals. The diet should contain less bulk and more concentrated food, with more meat (raw or cooked) or fish. Her milk intake should also be increased. As a precaution against calcium deficiency while nursing her litter, the food may be supplemented by additional calcium tablets with Vitamin D, which will also ensure that the puppies are born with sound bone and the foundations of good teeth.

In-whelp bitches vary considerably in their appetites. For the first four weeks she should not be given any increase in quantity, just quality. But from six weeks or so, the food should be increased slightly and is best then given as two separate meals. Exercise is most important and she should have her usual exercise until she becomes heavy and is obviously feeling uncomfortable. Then it should be gentle but still regular and continued for as long as the bitch can take it. Do not let her turn into a "couch potato", though, as this will not benefit either her or the puppies.

It makes sense for your vet to check over your bitch about five weeks into her pregnancy. Should his services be needed later, he knows the bitch and will have seen her beforehand. It is also a good idea to clipper off her belly hair during the final week, as this will help the puppies to suckle more easily, as well as helping to keep the bitch clean underneath.

PREPARING FOR WHELPING

You will have already decided on the whelping area and, by the eighth week, you should have a whelping box set up, ideally a purpose-built model which incorporates a pig-rail, to lessen the likelihood of puppies being crushed by an over-zealous mother. The box should also have a hinged lid, to afford easy access and yet retain warmth. At this stage your bitch should be encouraged to sleep in the whelping box. She will probably be feeling less than agile and be happy to retire to such a secluded spot.

While the average gestation period in the dog is 63 days, bitches have been known to whelp up to four days early, or four days late, with no problems.

Close to the whelping box you will need some basic equipment including the following: an ample supply of towels for rubbing puppies dry and stimulating circulation; sterile scissors for cutting any umbilical cords which the bitch herself may not have severed; strong cotton for tying any umbilical cords which may still be bleeding; brandy – no, not for you, but a drop can be applied to the tongue of a puppy which may appear lifeless and it often performs miracles; a plentiful supply of newspaper for the floor of the box; and several sheets of the fleecy-type dog bedding which is readily available, as a sheet should be put on top of the newspapers to keep the pups warm and allow any fluids to drain through to the papers below. Be sure to have your vet's telephone number right by the whelping box, and advise him beforehand of her expected date of whelping.

THE ONSET OF WHELPING

Keep an eye on your bitch from the 58th day after mating, and if she begins to refuse food, she may be close to the first stages. She will become very restless and begin scratching up her bed, possibly moving about the house exploring all alternatives, so watch her closely. If your bitch is absolutely determined to whelp in another part of the house, and seems reluctant to use the whelping box, rather than force her into the box, let her have the first puppy in her chosen spot. Then you can move her and her firstborn into the box, when she will be so preoccupied with the new baby that she will soon settle and deliver the other puppies in the appropriate place.

Before the actual birth, the bitch will often pass a blackish membrane, or this may be only partially discharged. If no puppy appears within the hour after this happening, telephone your vet, as a shot of pituitrin may be necessary to advance the whelping. Should the bitch be visibly bearing down during this period, with no signs of any result, veterinary help should also be enlisted.

THE BIRTH

Puppies will generally be presented head first. In the event of a head being visible, yet delivery does not then advance, you can help by gently but firmly holding the head in a towel, and each time the bitch contracts, you can slowly try to move the puppy further out, using a side-to-side motion. This will normally succeed. In the event of a puppy's feet being presented first – a breech-birth – you should again resort to the "towel method" and gently try to ease the puppy away.

Normally the bitch will herself open the enclosing bag in which puppies are born, and proceed to eat the afterbirth and sever the umbilical cord. This may be distasteful to you, but it is perfectly natural and will aid in the cleansing of the bitch's system and help the entire whelping process. However, if you have removed a puppy manually, the bitch may be less inclined the open the bag, so you will have to assist – and quickly. Tear open the bag near the head, using your fingers, otherwise the puppy will drown. You will probably need to cut the umbilical cord on such a puppy, and do

so about two inches away from the tummy, tying with cotton to avoid any haemorrhaging.

Should a puppy be born which appears rather lifeless, using your finger place a drop of brandy on its tongue. This may help it to rally. If it does not, hold the puppy firmly in your hand, the head poking out between your thumb and forefinger, and swing it downwards several times. This may well cause the puppy to gasp and help it to start breathing. You should try this for ten minutes or more before giving up.

Bitches vary, but they can go up to twenty minutes between puppies, yet some turn out a family like shelling the proverbial peas. If your bitch proves to be one of the latter, you are lucky. If the bitch appears to still be straining but no further puppies arrive after an interval of one hour, the vet should be called, as there may be a puppy stuck, which could necessitate a Caesarean section or an administration of pituitrin.

POST-WHELPING

If there are no such problems, and your bitch appears to be contented and settled with her puppies, licking and nuzzling them close to her, the chances are that she has no further puppies left. She will be reluctant to leave her new clutch, but at this stage she should be taken outside and encouraged to relieve herself totally. Meanwhile, you will have the opportunity to clean the whelping box and replace both papers and fleecy bedding. It can be a help actually to fix the bedding in place using large-headed screws which can be easily removed. This will prevent the puppies from getting underneath it and the bitch accidentally

The litter will divide their time between eating and sleeping in the first couple of weeks.

lying on them and, when the puppies get older and are on their feet, it will give them much better grip than a bedding sheet which slips and slides underneath them.

Offer the bitch a drink of warm milk when she returns and, now that the new family is safely delivered, this is the time for you to think about increasing the quantity of her food. At one time many breeders would have administered extra calcium to the bitch, and may be cod-liver oil. However, today's advanced feeding regimes are such that any quality complete feed makes this unnecessary.

DEWCLAWS, NAILS AND EYES
Miniature Schnauzer puppies are born with dewclaws on their forelegs and occasionally on their hind legs too. These should always be removed, as they can cause injury if torn in later life. Generally, if the puppies are strong and healthy, the dewclaws should be removed at around three to five days of age. Either an experienced breeder or your vet will carry out this simple operation which causes minimal distress. You should have already decided whether or not you wish to have your puppies' tails docked, as is traditional for the breed. These days some vets refuse to do this, so be sure you are dealing with a docking vet long before the litter is due. Tails are usually docked at around four to five days.

Remember, too, that puppies' nails can be as sharp as needles, and so can hurt and damage the bitch when the puppies are suckling. It is important to keep the puppies' nails cut back as close as you dare when they are small. Also, cutting them really close as babies will slow down their natural growth in later life and make management of the foot so much easier.

Puppies are born blind and their eyes open from about ten days of age. At first the eyes are bluish and seem weak; sometimes they are rather stuck-up with matter, in which case just wipe them with warm water and cotton wool several times until they are clean and open.

THE BITCH'S DIET
Your bitch should, for the first week after labour, be given two meals daily; afterwards the meals can be increased in size but the total daily intake depends very much on the size of the litter.

120

Obviously a bitch nursing eight puppies is having to give much more of herself than a bitch nursing three, so here again, use common sense – the most valuable tool of the successful dog breeder!

WEANING

The puppies will be quite happy with mother's milk for the first three weeks of their life, but weaning should begin. This should, initially, involve offering the puppies an appropriate complete puppy porridge. This is easy to administer and highly palatable and most puppies take to it instantly. When beginning weaning, take the bitch away from the puppies for about two hours so that they get hungry but have no milk bar to turn to. Offer a little of the porridge by gently pushing the puppies' noses into a dish. They will soon get both the taste and the idea and will generally start lapping without any further encouragement. On the second day of weaning, give them two such

feeds and by the end of a week – when they are now four weeks old – they should be on three meals daily. At this stage a proprietary puppy meal, either canned or dried, can be introduced. If a canned food is being used, this should be very slightly warmed, as this will intensify the appetising odour. If a dried food is the choice, this should always be soaked in warm water or gravy for at least an hour before feeding.

When the puppies are five weeks old and happily eating their regular meals, they should gradually be weaned off their mother. Up until this age, it is recommended that the bitch still sleeps with them. However, beyond this age the bitch should be taken away at night. If she still has an obvious quantity of milk, she should be allowed to visit them at least three times a day until she begins to dry up. At six weeks she should be completely off the puppies and her milk should then dry up completely.

One way of making sure all the puppies get their fair share of food!

By the time the puppies are eight weeks old, they will be fully independent and ready to go to their new homes.

LEAVING HOME

By the time the puppies are eight weeks old, they should be eating four hearty meals a day. Their mother should be happy to leave them alone, and they should be running around, getting into all sorts of mischief and ready for their new homes. Most Miniature Schnauzers are ready to adapt to a new home at this age, and the sooner they go, the more readily they settle into a new routine.

Puppies will always need worming, especially for roundworms, and there are several straightforward and satisfactory worming procedures that can be carried out nowadays before the puppies leave for their new homes. Before they leave, the eye-check should also have been carried out on the puppies by a recognised panellist.

You will obviously advise new owners of the puppy's diet and it is advisable always to give them a quantity of that food so that there is no dramatic change in the puppy's feeding habits at this stressful time. Should the new owners choose to change the puppy's diet, it should be done very gradually.

Hopefully your puppies' new owners will have been carefully vetted, as you will want to be as sure as is possible that the puppies are going to give their adopted families as much pleasure as your bitch has given you. Do ask them to keep in touch, and each Christmas, when you receive those festive cards with photographs of what was once your baby playing with his new family, you will be so proud and happy. I also suspect that, if you really are hooked, you are already planning that next litter.

8 *HEALTH AND WELFARE*

The Miniature Schnauzer is a naturally healthy breed, free from major hereditary problems, other than the eye troubles which occurred earlier in the development of the breed, and it tends to be long-lived provided that it has adequate exercise and sensible diet. Miniatures enjoy their food and can run to obesity, so do please refrain from giving tidbits, other than when training. Miniatures will soon pile weight on if given the chance to over-indulge. Here are some hints on first aid, but if any condition persists, veterinary attention should always be sought.

ANAL GLANDS
A Miniature Schnauzer, fed on a correct diet, and exercised properly, will be unlikely to suffer from impacted anal glands. The symptoms are the licking or biting of the anal area, or at the root of the tail. The dog may drag its bottom along the ground in an attempt to ease the irritation. Also there may be a very noticeable foul smell coming from the anus. An experienced breeder or vet will be able to express the glands which have become impacted, releasing the foul-smelling brown discharge. It is important to have the glands emptied as soon as the problem appears, as lack of attention could lead to a subsequent anal abscess.

BITES
Should your Miniature be bitten by another dog, or any animal, the severity of the wound should be assessed immediately. Antibiotic powder should always be kept in the first aid kit, the wound should be washed and a mild antiseptic applied, and then a coating of the powder. Obviously, if there is a deep wound, and bleeding is excessive, a visit to the vet is essential.

BURNS AND SCALDS
Burns and scalds can be treated with an ice pack to bring down the temperature; as a substitute a large packet of frozen peas wrapped in a towel will suffice. Proprietary sprays can be easily obtained from any pharmacist and used accordingly. Obviously, treatment will depend on the affected area, and a badly

A family group owned by breed specialist Carolyn Craig. The Miniature Schnauzer is a healthy breed and, with the correct care, most will live to a good age.

Photo: Derek Homewood, West Sussex.

scalded head, for example, should be dealt with by the vet after a cold compress has been applied.

CHOKING

The utmost care should be exercised when giving your Miniature Schnauzer any kind of toys, edible or otherwise, and items which are so small that they may be swallowed should always be avoided. Sometimes the popular hide chews can become very soft and can be swallowed, causing a blockage. Immediate examination should reveal whether or not the obstruction can be retrieved manually. If it is too far down the throat, it is advisable to try to push it even further down, and then follow this with a large piece of dry bread. The dog should swallow this automatically and, hopefully, the chew will then gradually be digested.

COUGHING

What is commonly referred to as "kennel cough" should really be re-named "canine cough" as it is by no means restricted to kennel dogs. One dog can easily contract a contagious cough simply by meeting another in the local park. The symptoms are a rasping cough, often accompanied by the impression of choking or retching, resulting in a little froth being brought up. Unless the dog is noticeably poorly, refusing food, and much more lethargic than usual, a human expectorant can be administered using a syringe and this will aid speedy recovery. If the condition persists, and there is no improvement after two weeks, veterinary advice should be sought.

CUTS

Depending on the size and severity of such wounds, these should be treated as bites – see above. If a cut is so deep that flesh is visibly hanging, stitching will probably be necessary.

DIARRHOEA

There are various causes of diarrhoea including over-eating, bacterial infection, a sudden change of diet and stress. If your Miniature has very loose motions, food should not be given for twenty-four hours, just fluid, ideally boiled water with added glucose. Also arrowroot can be stirred in to speed recovery.

EAR MITES

You may notice that your Miniature is scratching at his ears constantly, and examination of the ears may reveal a brown discharge around the inner ear. This should be treated with one of the many proprietary cures available from vets or pet shops, either drops or powder. Initially, a cotton bud soaked in olive oil or liquid paraffin can be used if there is a build-up of wax, but be careful not to probe too deeply. The hair inside the Miniature's ears should always be regularly plucked out to keep the ear-canal free and well-ventilated.

FITS

Miniature Schnauzers do not generally suffer from fits, but occasionally these may occur, the symptoms being frothing at the mouth and convulsions. Leave the dog in a quiet, darkened room and obtain some bromide tablets from the pharmacist. These will help to sedate the dog. If the fits recur, obviously your vet must be consulted.

FLEAS AND LICE

Dogs will, from time to time, pick up fleas from other livestock. Fleas do not lay eggs actually on their host, but in surrounding areas, such as carpets, furniture etc. Fleas can be detected by brushing the hand against the lie of the coat and examining close to the skin. There will, invariably, be signs of flea-dirt, usually at the base of the tail or on the neck. A strong insecticidal shampoo should be used as directed, and treatment repeated one week later. Also, it is important to spray the home environment with a purpose-made product. Lice may be easier to treat, as the eggs are laid on the dog, usually behind the ears but they can be found all over the body area. They should be treated similarly.

HEAT STROKE

If a dog is suffering from heat stroke it will appear somewhat dazed, with a glassy look about the eyes, and may stagger around with a distinct lack of co-ordination. In such a case, the dog should be immersed in a bath of cold water, with ice packs added if possible, so that the temperature is reduced as quickly as possible.

LACK OF APPETITE

Miniature Schnauzers are generally enthusiastic doers, but when a puppy is teething, it may well go off its food. As this is a vital growing age, puppies should never be allowed to lose too much weight, as they will seldom get it back and will, more importantly, lose bone. Many puppies of that age will sooner eat a dried food which will relieve the soreness of the gums and help the new teeth through, rather like the human baby and its teething ring. Plenty of hard, chewable biscuits should be available, otherwise your teething puppy may resort to chewing the furniture!

LAMENESS

Often puppies who play rough can sustain mild injury to the shoulder which will result in slight lameness. Do not panic and rush off to the vet, who may try to convince you that your young dog has some dreadful hereditary condition which is the result of "in-breeding". The dog should be rested and given the minimum of exercise until it is sound again. Also, lameness may be the result of a cut pad, in which case examine the pads closely and, if a cut is detected, treat as a normal cut, as above. If the pad has a hair-line cut, a product such as "New Skin" can be painted over which will give external protection while the cut heals.

MISMATING

In the unlikely event of your in-season bitch getting mated by an intruder, it is essential that you take her to the vet for an injection which will prevent conception, but will prolong the season. You will, however, be extra vigilant this time, and ensure that the same thing does not happen again.

NAIL CUTS AND RIPS

If you cut your dog's nails too close to the quick, they may bleed profusely and cause great pain. To assist drying up and healing, a styptic pencil can be used in lesser cases, but if there is excessive bleeding you may have to resort to applying potassium permanganate. This will be effective but you will be prevented from showing a dog with brown feet for a week or so! Sometimes a dog will catch its nail in a fence or crate and I have to admit that, marvellous as they are, permanent car-crates can easily rip out a nail if a dog is allowed to jump up into the back of the car and happens to catch its foot on the edge, so it is best to lift the dog up into the crate. Dogs can also rip a nail when playing, if they happen to turn quickly and catch it. If the nail is badly damaged but still attached to the toe, it may be best to have it removed as this can be very painful. If the nail is ripped right out, there will be great distress initially, but gradually it will begin to grow back.

STINGS

Most dogs are naturally inquisitive and will find wasps and bees very interesting. If your dog should be stung by a bee, the sting should be removed and antiseptic applied. When the sting is in the mouth, it can prove dangerous if swelling is detected and veterinary help should be sought as soon as possible.

TARTAR

This is the hard, brownish-yellow material which builds up on the teeth and is full of harmful bacteria. Dried food, biscuit and even sensible bones can help to prevent this tartar from accumulating. In bad cases, especially when the tartar has gone unchecked, there is an unpleasant smell from the dog's breath. Indigestion will result and the dog may not feed properly. If neglected, serious infection can result around the roots of the teeth and major gum disorders may follow. It is therefore wise to check the state of the teeth and, if necessary, scale them regularly. If the tartar is only slight, a charcoal pencil can be used effectively; if, however, it has a hold, it is best to take your dog for a veterinary check-up.

TEAR STAINS
This is a fairly common problem in Miniature Schnauzers and is caused by an impaired outflow of tears, rather than their over-production. It is most probably associated with some degree of congenital closure of the drainage duct and the blockage of the duct opening. It would appear that, with age, this condition becomes less severe. It is best to keep the eyes clean and avoid any build-up of dry secretions in the corner of the eye. Bathing with water is all that is required, except in the most serious of cases, when veterinary opinion should be sought.

TRAVEL SICKNESS
It is quite common for dogs to salivate and even vomit a little when they first travel by car, but most will naturally grow out of it. It is best not to feed or water your Miniature Schnauzer before starting a journey if it does have a tendency to car sickness. Taking the puppy out and about at every opportunity when it is young is the best way to ensure trouble-free travel. Letting your dog sit in the car when it is stationary at home can also ease the problem. Be careful if administering travel sickness preparations, as some of these can have a mild sedative effect, and this is obviously not a good idea if you are going to a dog show.

VOMITING
Dogs frequently eat grass and will vomit as a result, though this may be mainly froth and the consumed grass. It is a natural process and a cleansing agent, and will not result in any harm. However, if the dog should have consumed a toxic plant, it can be more serious. The dog will try to vomit and may appear to go off its legs. In this case pour strong salt water down the dog's throat and encourage it to vomit further. If the symptoms persist, veterinary assistance is essential.

WORMS
Puppies, in particular, are susceptible to worms, mostly roundworms. Tapeworms can also occur, and these can prove a problem which is difficult to treat. Unless the head of the tapeworm is expelled, it will continue to grow again and again. It is always advisable to consult with your vet regarding a regular worming regime to prevent any possibility of tapeworm becoming established.

SPECIAL CONSIDERATIONS

EYE CONDITIONS
To a very limited degree both hereditary and congenital cataracts and Generalised Progressive Retinal Atrophy (PRA) have appeared in Miniature Schnauzers in Britain. These conditions are all detectable by a simple ophthalmoscopic examination by a veterinarian, and all are inherited through a simple autosomal recessive gene – which means it is not sex-linked. A cataract is any opacity of the lens. This can take many forms, with only some being hereditary, and these, again, vary in form and from breed to breed.

With the Hereditary Congenital Cataract found in the Miniature Schnauzer, both eyes are affected and give a similar appearance. It is usually not progressive and may first be recognised at a few weeks of age, as it is present from birth. The other form of hereditary cataracts typically starts at eight to ten weeks. Defective vision, and a cataract obvious to the naked human eye, are not apparent in the puppy until sometime between nine and eighteen months of age. Progression continues until the cataracts are total and the dog will be blind at between two to four years of age. Although the condition is quite painless, an operation may be required to restore vision, which is then usually adequate but limited.

With Generalised Progressive Retinal Atrophy, the retina appears to be functioning normally at birth and in early life, but it later begins to degenerate. In the Miniature Schnauzer the ophthalmic signs and defective vision appear between the ages of two to five years. This, too, is not a painful condition but it is relentless in its progress, at first causing defective vision and night blindness, and ultimately resulting in total blindness.

OPHTHALMIC EXAMINATIONS
Juvenile cataract was the first to show in the breed in the UK, and although few in numbers, this was enough to alert serious breeders to the importance of, and the need for, eye checks to be done on all stock, especially as the problem can be detected early.

Litters should be eye-examined before the puppies leave to go to their new homes, with all dogs and bitches being re-checked before they are used for breeding. It is also strongly recommended that breeding stock continue to be checked throughout their life, which will also cover later onset conditions. It is important that all examinations are carried out by an approved panellist. The ophthalmic examination is private, simple and straightforward and merely involves dilating eye-drops being placed in the eyes and then, some twenty minutes later, the examination is carried out.

As to PRA, which, unlike congenital cataracts, is not readily detectable at a young age, it is important that it should be checked for at around three to four years of age, especially in any breeding stock.

It was back in 1966 that the Kennel Club and the British Veterinarian Association first introduced a scheme to check PRA in Elkhounds. Some three years later this was extended to cover all breeds and, later still, it was further extended to include hereditary cataracts.

Under the scheme the examination is carried out by an approved panellist and the result – pass or fail – is then recorded on the animal's registration records at the Kennel Club, as well as subsequently being endorsed on the registration certificates of all progeny.

The response for Miniature Schnauzers has been good, especially in comparison with other breeds, a fact that has often been favourably commented on by the examining panellists over the years but, sadly, in more recent times, there has been a noticeable falling-off in the numbers being submitted for testing.

The importance of these checks being continued, and carried out in depth throughout the breed, and over the years and generations, cannot be over-emphasised. This is particularly important because we only have a small gene pool with the breed, and since the conditions are also carried by a recessive gene, this means the problem can remain hidden but carried on through several generations before making an appearance.

DNA TESTING

Researchers have already successfully found a DNA blood-test for PRA in Irish Setters, a breed that is also affected by the disease – but not in the same form as that found in the Miniature Schnauzer.

This genetic screening means that not only animals that will one day be affected by the disease can be identified but, equally, those that are carriers – which carry a copy of the mutant gene – will also be identified. DNA testing can be carried out at an early age, in fact as soon as it is possible to take the small blood sample required. This can be taken by your own veterinarian and then sent off to the laboratory. It is a very simple and straightforward procedure.

With the DNA screening it will be possible to eradicate the disease, which is not possible through clinical screening alone. This will prove a big advantage when dealing with a late-onset disease like PRA as, without screening, a dog or bitch could have been used for breeding (however unwittingly) before the disease became clinically evident, and it would have been passed on to some of the progeny. No dog or bitch with an inherited problem should ever be bred from.

Research work on the PRA condition is currently being undertaken in the UK by Dr Simon Petersen Jones, D. Vet. Med. DV Ophthalm. Dip. FCVO, MRCVS, the chief panellist for the KC/BVA scheme, and his team at Cambridge University.

The American Miniature Schnauzer Club and its members are also deeply involved in supporting current research into eye diseases that affect the Miniature Schnauzer, particularly PRA, and it is hoped that, through this research in America and Britain, a DNA blood test will be developed for PRA in Miniature Schnauzers.

In the UK the breed clubs, like the American breed club, encourages an open exchange of information and also holds regular ophthalmoscopic examinations by a panellist for cataracts and PRA, all of which are detectable on close examination before any clinical signs are noted.

With congenital cataract it is important to appreciate that all puppies should be examined, not just those that may be destined for show or breeding, as just one affected puppy confirms that both parents are either affected or carriers. The other important factor is that, should cataracts develop later, then an earlier examination will aid the definitive diagnosis of cataract type.

INHERITANCE OF RECESSIVE DISEASE

With the eye problems in the Miniature Schnauzer, as we have seen, their mode of inheritance is via the simple recessive manner, which means that in order to be affected by the disease, a copy of the faulty gene must be inherited from *both* parents. If the dog or bitch inherits only one faulty gene then it will not be clinically affected itself but it does inherit the ability to pass on the disease. This is known as being a carrier.).

When two carriers are bred together, then an average of 25 per cent of their progeny will inherit two faulty genes and develop the disease. These are known as 'affected'. 50 per cent will inherit one good and one bad gene and be carriers like their parents, but the other 25 per cent will inherit two good genes and so have no problem nor pass on the disease. These are known as 'clear'.

If an affected is bred to a clear then all their progeny will be carriers. If an affected is bred to a carrier then half of their progeny will be affected and half carriers. If a clear is bred to a carrier then half of their progeny will be carriers but half will be clear.

At present, when an affected animal is detected, doubt is cast on the status of all related animals, some of which, although clinically unaffected, may carry the disease, so the importance of being able to recognise any carriers through DNA testing can clearly be seen. The ability to avoid breeding two carriers together means no affected animals need be born.

EAR CROPPING
Natural ears vary in size, structure and carriage. Cropping them is not always just a matter of fashion. If it is legal, and if it concerns a future showdog, it is often necessary. It changes the dog's expression, makes the neck and head look longer and cleaner and it also makes the whole dog more impressive.

It is usually done between eight and twelve weeks of age but it can be carried out later if required. The length and shape of the ears should be in proportion to the head, for the whole purpose of ear cropping is to give the best look to the dog.

After having their ears cropped the puppies can stay and play together, provided everything is kept clean and the edges of the ears are taken care of with an antiseptic ointment. However, if the puppies start scratching or licking each other's ears, it would be necessary to put collars on them. Puppies easily get used to them, and they do not keep them from eating, drinking or playing.

After a couple of days the stitches are taken out. The ears heal very quickly and are taped to the head, or the tips are simply taped or glued together, to make them stand perfectly. This is very easy to achieve with our Miniatures. If the whole procedure is done responsibly by a professional and treated properly, it does not harm the puppy in any way.

Some people think puppies will be reluctant about having their ears cleaned or groomed later on in life because of the 'cropping discomfort', but if one does it gently, little by little, the way grooming should always be done whether the ears are cropped or uncropped, they will not like it or dislike it any more than normal.

9 INFLUENTIAL KENNELS IN BRITAIN

Although this chapter details the leading UK kennels, it also illustrates the international influences which have affected the development of the Miniature Schnauzer.

In 1957 Donald Becker imported Dondeau Handful's Englan from Miss Gene Simmonds' Handful kennel in the USA. He was a son of Am. Ch. Dorem Original and Am. Ch. Handfuls Pheasant. Being cropped, he was never shown in the UK, but he did produce a Champion, in the home-bred Ch. Dondeau Handicap when mated to Dondeau Humbug, a daughter of Ch. Dondeau Helios and his half-sister, Ch. Dondeau Haphazard.

Two other breed enthusiasts from the early post-war days were Mrs Hardy (Ydrah) and Mrs Reynolds (Jovinus) who both, either separately or jointly, had several Champions. Mrs Reynolds was particularly interested in blacks, importing the Italian-bred Ch. Jovinus Malya Swanee from Mrs Pozzi. He was the first post-war black to make his title and was also to win Best in Show at the Miniature Club's Specialty in 1963, the

second time for Mrs Reynolds to do this with a black. Her first success had been in 1961 with the bitch, Jovinus Risotto, under Schnauzer Specialist Mrs Board. Risotto was to become the dam of the first post-war British-bred black Champion, Jovinus Replica. Sired by Ch. Malya Swanee, she was made up in 1969. In that same year Mrs Reynolds imported the pepper-and-salt dog, Ch. Dayan del Tomese, who was to make his British title. Although bred in Italy by Marisa Brivio Chellini, he enjoyed an Anglo-American background, as his sire was Jovinus Roundabout, a grandson of Risepark Northern Cockade and Roundway Anklet, while his dam was the American-bred Italian Ch. Shorlaine Doreli.

Tom and Katy Gately, well-known American handlers, sent two Miniatures from the USA into Britain who were to be very important. The first, in 1952, was the extrovert showman and cleverly named Ch. Wilkern Tony From America. He came over to the famous all-rounder judge Mrs Josephine Creasy of Roundway Wire Fox Terrier fame. Some time later, in 1967 in fact, the second import, Ch. Pinchpenny Luke of Gayterry, joined Mrs Crowe's Deltones. Tony carried much of the Dorem blood as well as Marienhof and Ledahof. He was highly successful at breed level and he also won the huge Non-Sporting Group at the 1954 WELKS show under the late, great Leo Wilson, the first Miniature Schnauzer to secure such a win. He also won several Bests in Show at toughly-contested Open all breeds shows. Although he sired two Champion males, Ch. Roundway Kelpie of Impstown and Ch. Jovinus Roxburgh, it is possibly through two bitches in particular that his blood was most influential. His mating to the American-bred Phil-Mar Ritzy Lady (Am. Ch. Dorem Tribute ex Am. Ch. Phil-Mar Lucky Lady) produced Roundway Antonia. She in turn was mated to Ch. Deltone Deldiablo (a son of Ch. Deltone Deloklahoma and Deltone Delsanta Monica). From this union came the littermates Roundway Anthony and Roundway Angelface. These two were mated together and produced Roundway Anklet, the top producing bitch to date in the breed, with six Champions to her credit – three to the Pickwick Pepper son, Risepark Northern Cockade, and three to the American-bred Ch. Risepark Bon-Ell Taurus. Anklet offspring appear in the back pedigrees of many of today's major winners.

THE STICKY WICKET PROGENY
When Pamela Cross-Stern (daughter of the famous All-Rounder, Fred Cross) returned to England from living in the USA, she brought three of her American Champions with her: Am. Ch. Nicomur

Chasseur, his son Am. Ch. Sternroc Sticky Wicket, and the bitch Am. Ch. Flinthill Glitterbug. All produced Champions, but it was those by Sticky Wicket that were to most influence the breed, mainly through his matings to Eastwight and Gosmore bitches. Gosmore was the kennel of Audrey Dallison, one of the most successful of British exhibitors over a number of years, finishing Champions in a variety of different breeds but notably Terriers. Mrs Dallison made up her first Miniature in 1960, Ch. Gosmore Peach Brandy, a daughter of Ch. Deltone Deldiablo who was strong in Roundway breeding on her dam's side.

For the Sticky Wicket progeny, Mrs Dallison developed a cricketing theme for her names which proved to be a clever move, and with their successes in the show ring they certainly drew attention to the individual dogs and the breed. Ch. Gosmore Hat Trick won a total of 17 CCs and with these held the bitch record for some twelve years, while Ch. Gosmore Opening Batsman (also by Sticky Wicket) with his 24 CCs held the dog record for nearly fifteen. Batsman was the sire of Ch. Rownhams Batman (co-owned by Mrs Quigley and Miss Morrison-Bell) and it was through his mating to Ch. Eastwight Sea Nymph that the Sticky Wicket line has continued in the breed, as they produced Ch. Eastwight Sea Sprite.

Another American-bred, Ch. Rannoch Dune Randolph (imported by Doug Appleton), was mated to Ch. Deltone Destelle, and produced Deltone Cherokee whose grand-daughters, Risepark Hapenny Breeze, Deltone Delsanta Monica and Ch. Deltone

Delsanta Barbara, all carried the breeding forward into the pedigrees of many of the Champions and notable producers of the sixties and seventies.

Later Douglas Appleton imported the Canadian-bred Appeline Cosburn's Pickwick Peppers. With his background of Benrook, Dorem, Ledahof and Marienhof breeding, he was to tie in well with bloodlines that were already being developed in the UK. Pepper not only sired several Champions, particularly for Miss Morrison-Bell's Eastwight kennel, but several Champion producers as well. Sadly he did not quarantine well and was never shown, living out his life with my own Riseparks, and proving to be a sweet-natured dog with a most delightful temperament, which he passed on to all his puppies.

Ch. Eastwight Sea-Fantasy (left) and Ch. Rownhams Batman.
Owned by Miss P. Morrison-Bell.
Photo: Joy Warren.

EASTWIGHT

Pamela Morrison-Bell's first Champion, Eastwight Sea Nymph, was a grand-daughter of Ch. Wilkern Tony through her sire, Rownhams Cavalier, so many more Champions in the breed are also able to trace back to Tony through her. Miss Morrison-Bell joined the breed ranks in the Ch. Deltone Appeline Doughboy era, through his daughter, Deltone Delnevada, who was by the American-bred Ch. Rannoch Dune Randolph of Appeline out of Ch. Dondeau Harvest Moon, a daughter of Ch. Dondeau Hamerica. Keeping mainly within its own confines over the decades, Eastwight has proved to be a top-producing kennel with some thirty British and fifteen overseas Champions to date. Almost all of these (twenty-six in fact) have been home-bred and come down through Deltone Delmanhatton's

two producing daughters, Ch. Eastwight Sea Nymph (by Rownhams Cavalier) and Ch. Eastwight Spillikins (by Ch. Deltone Deldiablo). Spillikins produced two Champions in Ch. Rownhams Eastwight Sea Lawyer (by Cavalier) and Ch. Eastwight Sea Gala (by the Canadian bred Appeline Cosburn's Pickwick Peppers).

Ch. Eastwight Sea Nymph proved especially influential through her three Champion daughters, Ch. Eastwight Sea Sprite (by Am. Ch. Sternroc Sticky Wicket) and Ch. Eastwight Sea Enchantress and Ch. Eastwight Sea Music (both by Pickwick Peppers). Ch. Sea Enchantress, when mated to Ch. Rownhams Batman (a son of Opening Batsman and Sea Music), produced Ch. Eastwight Sea Fantasy. When Fantasy was then mated to Ch. Eastwight Sea Gnome (Ch. Rownhams Eastwight Sea Lawyer ex Ch. Eastwight Sea Pixie), she produced Ch. Eastwight Sea Enchantment who, in turn, was then mated to Ch. Buffels All American Boy of Deansgate and produced the Champion brother and sister, Eastwight Sea Yank and Eastwight Sea Charmer, thus giving the kennel five Champion bitches in direct line. A repeat mating produced Ch. Eastwight Sea Spirit. Although the line of Champions was broken, the influence of Sea Nymph continued, as Ch. Sea Yank was mated to Betty and Archie Fletcher's first Champion, Deansgate Short and Sweet, to produce Ch. Arbey Yankee Doodle and Ch. Arbey Yankee Starlet. He also sired Ch. Sea Gamble of Eastwight, one of the very few Eastwight Champions not bred at the home kennel. Ch. Sea Fantasy, with four Champions – Sea Enchantment, Sea Goblin and Sea Lord (by Ch. Sea Gnome) and Sea Fancy (by Am. Ch. Travelmor's Fantazio) is to date the breed's third top-producing bitch, along with Gosmore Peaches and Cream.

The Eastwights have the added interest of carrying the recessive gene for the black and silver colour, and the kennel has played an important part in its progress and recognition over the decades. The cleverly named Sea Voyager (Ch. Rownhams Batman ex Ch. Eastwight Sea Enchantress) was, perhaps, the first to create real interest in the colour. Born in 1967, he was exported to Mrs Joanna Griggs of the Sylva Sprite kennel in Canada, for whom he became Can. Ch. Eastwight Sea Voyager CD – incidentally, the first

uncropped Miniature Champion in Canada. He had a strong influence on the colour in North America, his blood being carried by many of the top black and silver winners and producers, especially through his son, Am. Can. Ch. Sylva Sprite Snowy Mittens, the first black and silver to hold both titles. He sired at least eight Champions. Another son, Sylva Sprite Entity, went to Switzerland and strongly influenced the black and silvers in Europe.

In 1986 Pam and Dave Wick made up Ch. Qassaba Tia Christel, a daughter of Eastwight Sea Wizard (Ch. Eastwight Sea Swank ex Ch. Sea Gamble of Eastwight) and Ripplevale Frosty Kismet of Qassaba (Rownhams Impressario ex Ripplevale Frosty Ice). She was the first black and silver Champion in Britain. The latest Eastwight title holder, Ch. Eastwight Sea Mannikin, who made his crown in 1993, is actually Miss Morrison-Bell's first black and silver Champion. Both his parents, Eastwight Sea Clown and Eastwight Sea Flower, trace back to Ch. Sea Goblin and Ch. Sea Charmer.

The second British black and silver Champion was the male, Ch. Ashwick The Real McCoy, a son of Tia Christel and Proscenium Bilbo Baggins, bred by the Wicks and finished in 1991 by his owner, Marilyn Price.

The Wicks also bred the pepper and salt male Ch. Ashwick Mr. Pickwick, a son of the American-bred Ch. Travelmors US Mail and their Ch. Deansgate Aunty Nuff of Ashwick, who was exported to Anders Hassen of Norway, where he became a National and International Champion and also made some good wins, as well as being a significant and trend-setting stud there.

ROWNHAMS
Before she became interested in Miniature Schnauzers, Miss Elaine Ashworth (now Mrs Quigley) was well-known and successful with Kerry Blue Terriers and several other breeds. Starting with two Dondeau litter sisters who traced back to the German-bred Dondeau Favorit Heinzelmannchen, these formed the basis of her early breeding, but it was not until she introduced the blood of the American-bred Ch. Wilkern Tony into her breeding programme that Rownhams began to be established, notably through Rownhams Cavalier, the Tony son who played a prominent part in the breed's progress.

Elaine Quigley's first Champion in the breed was Ch. Eastwight Sea Music, one of two Champion daughters of Ch. Eastwight Sea Nymph and Appeline Cosburn's Pickwick Peppers. Made up in 1966, she in turn produced Ch. Rownhams Susique and Ch. Rownhams Heron to Ch. Rownhams Eastwight Sea Lawyer, another Cavalier son but this time out of Ch. Eastwight Spillikins. Ch. Rownhams Batman was Sea Music's third Champion, but he was by Ch. Gosmore Opening Batsman. Like his sire, who produced three Champions, Batman proved a producing sire and, in fact, went one better by siring four title-holders, all – as was the case with his sire – from different bitches. Both Ch. Heron and Ch. Batman were co-owned by Miss Morrison-Bell and Mrs Quigley.

Ch. Eastwight Sea Fantasy, a Batman daughter, also produced three Champions, all to Ch. Eastwight Sea Gnome, a son of Ch. Sea Lawyer, which put them both into the top-producer ratings. Their daughter, Ch. Eastwight Sea Enchantment, was in turn a top producer with three Champions, as detailed in the Eastwight kennel's profile. Mrs Quigley has always been a strong supporter of the black and silver colour, and encouraged its acceptance. Her Rownhams Impressario, having a mainly Eastwight background, is behind many of the present day black and silvers in Britain. He was also the first of his colour to be awarded a Challenge Certificate, this being at Darlington in 1982 under judge Phillip Bagshaw who also made him Best of Breed.

SETTNOR
It was Ch. Quarrydene Frances of Settnor who introduced Mrs Dorothy Owen to the breed and proved to be a very good winner for her, especially at the northern all breeds Open Shows where she frequently won Best in Show. Ch. Frances was to produce Rhianfa San Jose of Settnor and Ch. San Marta of Settnor when mated to Ch. Risepark Happy Fella. San Marta was, in turn, to produce Ch. San Martinique of Settnor, a top-winning bitch with 10 CCs, when mated to Ch. Sceptre of Settnor (a son of Mrs Owen's Quarrydene Flicka of Settnor). Another Sceptre daughter, Seamstress, when mated to Ch. Gosmore Opening Batsman, produced a top-winning bitch for Mrs Dallison in Ch. Gosmore Miss Catch. Mrs Owen was to own two more Champions, bred by Mrs Milsom, the sisters Ch. Scissors of Settnor and Ch. Snippet of Settnor. The latter, when mated to Ch. Gosmore Opening Batsman, produced Ch.

Gosmore Silverstar of Settnor, another title-maker shown by Vincent Mitchell for Mrs Dallison. Rhianfa San Jose of Settnor, when mated to Risepark Roundway Autograph, a Northern Cockade/Anklet son, produced the littermates Ch. San Jolyon of Settnor and Ch. San Josephine of Settnor. Josephine was then mated to Ch. Sceptre to produce Ch. Sao Selena of Settnor, made up in 1974 and the last Champion bred and shown by Mrs Owen. Ch. Sao Selena was the dam of Settnor Selenda, owned by Tom Fernyhough, and to his Ch. Fearnought of Fernery she produced Ch. Fernery Fantastic, who proved to be a significant stud as the sire of Fred and Phyl Morley's Ch. Castilla Linaguido, to date the breed's most winning dog or bitch. A repeat of this mating resulted in the Morleys' Ch. Regalada in Castilla. In total, Mrs Owen's Settnor affix was borne by eleven Miniature Schnauzer Champions.

RISEPARK

The author is another who was first attracted to the breed in the Doughboy era and started with two of his puppies, Deltone Delouisiana and, later, Ch. Deltone Delaware, who made his title in 1955.

He also qualified for his Junior Warrant, only the second Miniature to do so. Mated together, these two produced Risepark Ha'penny Breeze, the first to carry the affix and the dam of two Champions.

The Risepark dogs have played a significant part in the breed's progress, particularly through a series of American-bred imports which began with the Am. Ch. Mutiny I'm Grumpy

Too son, Ch. Risepark Bon-Ell Taurus, who finished in 1969.

Through his mating to the top-producing Roundway Anklet came his most influential son, Ch. Risepark Toreador, who, in turn, sired Pam Radford and Dorrie Clarke's Ch. Iccabod Chervil, the sire of seven Champions including Ch. Castilla Zambra, the dam of Ch. Castilla Linajudo, one of the breed's all-time greats, and Ch. Castilla Diamante who, like her dam, was a significant producer. Chervil also sired Ch. Iccabod Mixed Herbs, another who enjoyed top-producing status and who was to prove an influential stud for several of the kennels emerging at that time.

Interestingly, the studs that have been available at Risepark over the years, from the very first home-bred Ch. Risepark Happy Fella, have all sired both Champions and Champion-producers. The Canadian-bred Appeline Cosburn's Pickwick Peppers sired three, all to Champion Eastwight bitches. A son, Risepark Northern Cockade (bred by Mr Wilkinson Snr.) out of the Ch. Delaware/Delouisiana daughter, Risepark Northern Lass, sired four Champions, three out of the top producer Roundway Anklet and one out of Risepark Pennyluck. Anklet was also the dam of three of the five Champion offspring of the American-bred Ch. Risepark Bon-Ell Taurus, of which two – the littermates Ch. Sonshea Silver Bullette (owned by Sonny and Sheila Dawe) and Ch. Risepark Toreador, proved to be particularly successful.

Bullette was the dam of Ch. Sonshea Sweet Talk at Risepark, while the third Champion from the combination of

Ch. Risepark The Leading Lady (American-bred Ch. Risepark Bon-Ell Taurus ex Roundway Anklet). Bred & owned by Peter Newman. Finished in 1972 and would still do well today. Photo: Anne Roslin-Williams.

Taurus and Anklet, Ch. Risepark The Leading Lady, was the dam of Barry and Jean Day's Ch. Risepark Crown Prince, winner of Best Puppy in Show at Leicester in 1976 and a 'Babychamp' with three CCs before he was a year old. He made his title at Crufts in 1977 with Best of Breed under Audrey Dallison.

Another top producing sire was Ch. Jidjis Min Cato at Risepark, bred in Sweden by the well-known all-rounder judge, Marianne Fürst-Danielson, from Am. Ch. Starfire Criterion Landmark (who had such a sparkling career Stateside in the hands of Ric Chashoudian) out of Catalanta Miss Lissette, a Toreador daughter sent over to Sweden by Sid and Gill Saville. Min Cato was to sire eight Champions in all, and his son, Ch. Catalanta True Luck of Risepark (out of Catalanta Little Sparkle, a sister to Lissette) was to carry on the good work as the sire of a further three Champions, which included Mr and Mrs Dobson's Ch. Castilla Real Quatro at Nosbod, the dam of the 1983 'Pup of the Year' finalist, Nosbod Daniel of Deansgate (Ch.), a son of Ch. Castilla Linajudo.

Since that time the breed has enjoyed further 'Pup of the Year' successes, and the Risepark kennel has had three Miniatures competing in the Finals over the years – Maid for Us at Risepark, Ch. Sonshea Call Me Mister Risepark and Ch. Risepark Our Miss Daisy. The sire of Maid For Us at Risepark, Ch. Irrenhaus Impact at Risepark, really stamped his mark as a sire; when Ch. Risepark Chase The Ribbons made her title, she was his tenth Champion, making him the first Miniature sire to achieve this. One of the highlights of Impact's show career, and a success that was very special to the author, was winning Best in Show at the Schnauzer Club's Championship show under the late, much respected, R.M. James, when his daughter, Ch. Castilla Diamante, also won the Bitch CC.

Aptly named and American-bred, Ch. Irrenhaus Impact at Risepark was an impressive dog, particularly on the move, and he certainly had the stamp of his breeding which he, in turn, transmitted to his many descendants. He sired eleven Champions and he and the other American-bred male, Pam Radford and Dorrie Clarke's Ch. Travelmors US Mail, proved a formidable pair of stud dogs. They and their progeny all tied in well with each other and helped to consolidate the type and sturdiness which the earlier American imports had already introduced into the breed in Britain. Among Impact's offspring, the bitches Ch. Castilla Diamante, Ch.

Starlite Blend at Risepark, Ch. Brentella Northern Luck and Ch. Malenda Miscanthus are all making their mark in the breed as producers, as indeed is the Impact son, Ch. Irish Ch. Risepark Here Comes Charlie.

The most recent American-bred male to join Risepark is Ch. Repetitions Favorite Son, sired by Am. Ch. Rampage's Representative. Although only at restricted stud, he too is proving to be an influential sire. His first titled son, Ch. Risepark Firm Favorite, stamps his type and outline, and is already the sire of Paul Scanlon and Monica Betts' Irish and UK Ch. Risepark Favorite Fella, the most-winning Miniature ever to date in the Irish Republic – all achieved before his second birthday. This exciting young dog started his "mainland" campaign off well in 1997 by taking Best of Breed at Manchester, then returning home to top a strong group at the St. Patrick's Day show. Although Barry Day's Ch. Risepark Crown Prince had made his title in 1977, it was the Ch. Castilla Diamante daughter, Ch. Iccabod Skydancer at Risepark, that gave the Newman and Day partnership their first Champion in 1986.

The Pup of the Year finalist, Ch. Sonshea Call Me Mister Risepark, bred by Sheila and Sonny Dawe, was by Ch. Irish Ch. Risepark Here Comes Charlie out of Daylorn Cephius at Sonshea, another daughter of Ch. Iccabod Mixed Herbs. He is the partnership's most winning Miniature to date, with two Bests in Show at general Championship shows, and he shares the honour with his paternal grandsire, Ch. Castilla Linajudo, of being the breed's only Crufts Group winners. Ch. Risepark Our Miss Daisy

had a spectacular, if short, show career during which she won ten CCs and a Group, while Maid For Us at Risepark is the dam of Shaune Frost and David Bates' Ch. Risepark Remember Me at Armorique, the top bitch of 1992, dual Specialty winner, and also a Champions Stakes finalist.

ICCABOD
The partnership of Miss Pam Radford and Mrs Dorrie Clarke has been consistently successful at the highest level, with their Iccabod Miniatures having a profound influence on the breed at large, particularly during the seventies and eighties. Their first Champion was Ch. Iccabod Chervil (by Ch. Risepark Toreador out of Iccabod Solitaire, who enjoyed a Risepark, Deltone and Dondeau background), made up in 1974. He went on to become a leading sire, with seven Champions to his credit. These included Fred and Phyl Morley's Ch. Castilla Zambra (out of Castilla Golosina, a Roundway Anklet daughter) and Barbara and Derek Clark's Ch. Iccabod Mixed Herbs (out of the imported American-bred Ch. Travelmor's From US To You).

Both Zambra and Mixed Herbs also became influential producers. Zambra became the dam of Ch. Castilla Linajudo (by Ch. Fernery Fantastic) and also of the partnership's bitch, Ch. Castilla Diamante (by Ch. Irrenhaus Impact at Risepark). Diamante, a dual Group winner in 1983, became a top producer with three Champions, while Linajudo became the breed's top winner and also sired two Champions. The Group-winning Ch. Iccabod Mixed Herbs also went on to become a great sire with

American-bred Ch. Travelmors from US to You (Am. Ch. Skyrockets Travelmor ex Am. Ch. Reflections Lively Image). Bred by Bill Moore, owned by Mesdames Radford & Clarke. A previous bitch Challenge Certificate record holder, she won at both Club Specialty Shows and went Best in Show at Driffield Championship show in 1982. The first Miniature bitch to win a Best in Show at a British General Championship Show.

Ch. Travelmors US Mail: An outstanding show dog and stud, currently the Number One sire with 17 Champions to his credit.

Photo: Pearce.

eight title-holders to his credit, which includes the breed's one-time bitch record holder, Tracy and Peter Slingsby's home-bred Ch. Samavai Steps Out.

The partnership imported two cleverly-named Miniatures from the Travelmor kennel in the USA. Firstly, in 1981, the bitch Ch. Travelmors From US To You (Am. Ch. Skyrockets Travel More ex Am. Ch. Reflections Lively Image) arrived, and she became the first bitch of the breed to win Best in Show at a general Championship show in Britain. This she did at Driffield in 1982, where the breed was judged by Catherine Sutton, the Group by Ben Johnson, and

Best in Show by Rita Price-Jones. She also competed in the 1983 Contest of Champions. She made her title in three straight shows, and in all won 19 CCs, all under different judges, being the breed's top winning bitch until she was displaced by her grand-daughter, the Mixed Herbs-sired Ch. Samavai Steps Out.

The other import was the dog, Ch. Travelmors US Mail (Am. Ch. Skylines Blue Spruce ex Am. Ch. Reflections Lively Image), who was released from quarantine in July 1983. In September the following year he won Best in Show at Birmingham City under Terry Thorn,

139

who had also judged the Group, the breed that day being judged by another much-respected all-rounder, Percy Whitaker. That same year he also won Best in Show at the Utility Breeds show under Ann Wynyard. Among his other notable wins during the year were Best in Show at the Miniature Club's Silver Jubilee show, judged by the club's President, Miss Morrison-Bell, and at the Schnauzer Club's show under Mrs Quigley. His total of 14 CCs could have been added to considerably had the partners wished to campaign him extensively.

He also won a round of the Pedigree Chum Champion Stakes competition three years in succession – in 1984 at Richmond under Richard Keenan, in 1985 at the LKA under Terry Thorn, and in 1986 on his home ground at Peterborough under Bill Pinches. In 1986 he was Runner-Up in the nationwide Pedigree Chum/Dog World Stud Dog competition for all breeds, being represented by ten different Certificate winners, five of whom were to go on and become Champions. To date "Ollie" is the breed's leading stud dog with 17 Champions to his credit, his last being Glenys Allen's Ch. Malenda Mignotte, made up at Windsor under Shaune Frost in 1997.

The two imports were only mated together once and from this union the partners kept Ch. Iccabod Travellers Tail, who sired six Champions – three for Trawest (Miss Pat Stewart), two for Wrendas (Elaine and Roger Ward) and one for Katar (Mrs Pat Kidd). In 1991 the partners made up Ch. Iccabod Country Style, a home-bred daughter of Iccabod Close Encounter at Renlott (Ch. Irrenhaus Impact at Risepark ex Ch. Travelmors From US To You) and Ch. Risepark Maid To Order (Ch. Travelmors US Mail ex Ch. Irrenhaus Aims To Please Risepark), which brought together as grandparents the two Travelmors and the two Irrenhaus imports. She was from one of the last litters the partners bred and was also the last Iccabod to grace the show ring. Their affix has been one of the most successful and respected in the breed.

ARMORIQUE

Shaune Frost and David Bates have enjoyed some really spectacular and outstanding wins with their Miniatures, which really all began when they first started to show Ch. Iccabod Olympic Gold in 1989. This son of Ch. Malenda Masterblend at Risepark and Ch. Iccabod Skylark (one of three Champions from the mating of Ch. Castilla Diamante to Ch. Travelmors US Mail) won three CCs, all with Best of Breed, as a puppy and was, not surprisingly, the breed's top puppy and

Ch. Maid For Gold at Armorique (Ch. Iccabod Olympic Gold ex Sonshea Golden Streamers). Bred by Ivan Sergant, owned by Messrs Frost & Bates. The top-winning Miniature bitch in England with 34 Challenge Certificates, ten Groups and two Bests in Show to her credit.

Photo: Russell Fine Art.

went on to be the leading Miniature in both 1990 and 1991. A highlight win was his Best in Show at Darlington in 1990, where he won the breed under Douglas Wilkinson, the Group under Ellis Hulme, and Best in Show under Jean Lanning. Ch. Risepark Remember Me to Armorique followed and she too gave the partnership some exciting wins, including the Champion Stakes at Birmingham City in 1992. In all she won ten CCs as well as going Best in Show at the Schnauzer Club's Championship show in the same year.

Ch. Maid for Gold with Armorique, Olympic Gold's daughter out of Sonshea Golden Streamers (sister to Ch. Sonshea Scarlett Streamers at Risepark and Ch. Sonshea Call Me Mister Risepark), was another who had a really spectacular career. She won the Pup of the Year finals under Ann Argyle in 1993 and is one of the few to win the finals when actually still a puppy. Earlier she had shot to fame on the day she qualified for the finals at the end-of-the-year LKA show, by not only taking this great win but also Best in Show under Albert Wight. She was also, later, to win Best in Show at the Utility Breeds Championship show, and at both the Miniature and Northern Club Championships as well. Like her sire, she too won Best of Breed at Crufts – in both 1994 and 1996 – taking Reserve in the Group at the former show

when she made her title. In all she won six Groups and stood Reserve on ten occasions. She won Reserve Best in Show at South Wales in 1995 and, with 34 CCs to her credit, she is the current bitch record holder. As a young dog, Ch. Risepark Mister Nice Guy with Armorique was campaigned along with Maid for Gold, and was the top winning male in 1994, winning 7 CCs. The partnership now has the added satisfaction of seeing Ch. Armorique Chase The Ace claim her crown in 1996, their first home-bred Champion.

MALENDA

Mrs Glenys Allen, who owns the Malenda Miniatures, became interested in the breed back in the early seventies and started with Catalanta Miss Lucy, bred by Sid and Gill Saville from Ch. Risepark Toreador and Catalanta Risepark Lucky Charm, a daughter of Ch. Risepark Bon Ell Taurus. She, along with her litter sister, Miss Lisette, were to prove a sound foundation and also play a significant part in the breed's progress. Miss Lucy produced two Champions when mated to the All American Boy son, Ch. Incheril For A' That. The dog, Ch. Malenda Tobermory of Risepark, won Best Puppy in Show at Bath in 1974 and went to Italy soon after making his title. His litter sister, Ch. Malenda Melisande, was mated to

Ch. Malenda Master Blend at Risepark (Ch. Iccabod Mixed Herbs ex Malenda Mint Imperial).
Bred by Mr & Mrs Allen, owned by Peter Newman & Barry Day.
Photo: Sally Anne Thompson.

the Swedish-bred Ch. Jidjis Min Cato of Risepark and, in turn, produced two Champions like her dam before her. Ch. Malenda Mimosa was Best of Breed at the Club Championship show of 1978, while Ch. Malenda Mimulus at Risepark had been the Puppy Stakes winner at Driffield the previous year. Malenda Mint Sauce, another from Miss Lucy but sired by Ch. Iccabod Chervil, was also mated to Min Cato and she too produced a brace of Champions in Ch. Malenda Mint Crisp and Ch. Malenda Moselle.

A daughter of Ch. Mimosa and Ch. Iccabod Chervil, Malenda Manda's Dream, produced Ch. Malenda Miscanthus, while Ch. Mint Crisp mated to Ch. Irrenhaus Impact of Risepark became the dam of Malenda Mint Imperial and Malenda Mistletoe. Mint Imperial was put to Ch. Iccabod Mixed Herbs to produce Ch. Malenda Mentha Mix and Ch. Malenda Master Blend at Risepark, and Mistletoe, mated to the same dog, produced Ch. Samavai Steps Out, Tracey Slingsby's one-time bitch record holder. In all she won nineteen CCs, her first coming as a minor puppy. She also won the bitch CC at Crufts three years in succession, the first along with her title and Best of Breed in 1990. She was again Best of Breed on the third occasion in 1992. Mentha Mix was the top winning bitch of 1988 and her brother, Master Blend, proved a successful sire.

Mint Imperial also had a litter to Ch. Iccabod Olympic Gold, which contained Ch. Malenda Moschatel. Ch. Mentha Mix was mated to Carolyn Craig's Ch. Balmar Silver Cracker to give Carolyn and her husband Malcolm their next

Champion, Ch. Malenda Mentha Santason. Ch. Malenda Masquerade, made up in 1995, was the 16th Champion for her sire, Ch. Travelmors US Mail, her dam – Malenda Mint Creme – being the same way bred as Ch. Mentha Mix, while Ch. Malenda Mignonette made up in 1997 and a Ch. Moschatel daughter is the seventeenth and last Champion for US Mail.

Although having only a small family of Miniatures, and just keeping bitches, and only breeding one or two litters a year – sometimes not even that – over the years Glenys Allen has shown herself to be a very clever breeder and very astute in her choice of stud dogs. Her line has remained within tight bounds, with the introduction of fresh blood coming through imports, most notably those brought in by Iccabod and Risepark. Perhaps this is best illustrated by the breeding of the littermates Ch. Mentha Mix and Ch. Master Blend and a third sibling who became a Champion overseas, these being the offspring of Ch. Iccabod Mixed Herbs and Malenda Mint Imperial. Over the years the Malenda Miniatures sent overseas have also done well, both in the show ring and as producers, almost all becoming Champions.

BRENTELLA
Douglas and Doreen Wilkinson, with the Brentella Miniatures, were introduced to the breed back in the early sixties when Mr Wilkinson Senior had, firstly, Risepark Northern Lass and then Ch. Risepark Karousel. When mated to the Canadian-bred Pickwick Peppers, Northern Lass produced Risepark Northern Cockade who sired three

Ch. Beaulea Light Blue (Am. Bred Ch. Travelmors US Mail ex Iccabod Jaywalker).Bred & owned by Dr. & Mrs Franklin. First Miniature to be finished by the breeders, an interesting combination of the American Travelmors lines, through US Mail and Ch. From US to You.

Roundway Champions bred by Mrs Creasy – Anchor, Annabelle and Applejack, all out of Roundway Anklet, the breed's current top producing bitch, with six Champions to her credit.

Northern Cockade has a place in the breed's history since his progeny particularly suited Ch. Risepark Bon Ell Taurus bitches, as well as the Roundway breeding. He is in the back pedigrees of many producers and winners of the era.

The Wilkinsons, in partnership with me, made up Ch. Risepark Scarlet Ribbons in 1966, but it was not until the eighties that they were able to become really involved with Miniatures, making up Ch. Brentella Northern Luck in 1984 and, in 1986, her litter brother, Ch. Brentella Northern Star. Although the Wilkinsons only breed occasionally, other Brentella Champions followed, including Northern Luck's daughter, Ch. Brentella Lucky Choice (by Ch. Travelmors US Mail) in 1988, while in 1985 Barry Day had made up Ch. Brentella Northern Encore (by Ch. Irrenhaus Impact at Risepark out of a daughter of Ch. Jidjis Min Cato of Risepark).

The Wilkinsons also enjoy the Irish show scene and have become regular exhibitors in the Republic. Their Ch. Irish Ch. Risepark Here Comes Charlie was the first Anglo-Irish Champion in the breed. They have also shown to her Irish title Maid Welcome at Brentella, and these two are the parents of the Brentellas currently being shown. A son, Ch. Brentella Del Boy, finished in 1996. A younger brother, Brentella Stormin Norman, was a finalist in the 1995 Irish Pup of the Year competition, and his sister Ch. Brentella Charlie Girl at Risepark, finished in 1997.

BEAULEA

Pat and Ray Franklin of the Beaulea Miniatures have quickly established a prominent position in the breed, with a strong hand in bitches based on their foundation bitch, Iccabod Jay Walker, a litter sister to Ch. Mixed Herbs. At the time they took out their affix in 1986, Jay Walker had the first of her three litters to Ch. Travelmors US Mail, with Beaulea High Society being the only bitch. High Society produced two Champions in Ch. Beaulea Blue Print and Ch. Beaulea Your Sensational, their latest to finish, which she did in 1996. The male, Blue Print, was sired by Beaulea Blue Chip, a son of the Spanish-bred Ch. Chipirrusquis Chipi at Kanix (a son of Int. Am. Ch. Sole Baye's John Henry) and out of Ch. Beaulea Light Blue, who was herself bred the same way as High Society. Sensational was similarly bred, being by Beaulea Just William, who was a son of Chipi and Jay Walker.

In Jay Walker's second litter, a dog

who became Ch. Beaulea Postscript went to Pam Radford and Dorrie Clarke (Iccabod), with the Franklins themselves keeping Ch. Beaulea Light Blue and her sister, High Mettled. Postscript and Light Blue won their titles in 1990 and High Mettled went on to win one CC and several Reserves. For two years running, 1988 and 1989, Jay Walker was the breed's top brood bitch.

Pat and Ray Franklin have enjoyed some really good wins in the breed and have established a recognisable type with their breeding. Although the suggestion has often been made to them that they should concentrate on showing just one or two dogs at a time, rather than their usual team, the Franklins prefer to show several at once, thus enjoying the pleasure and satisfaction of having all their dogs consistently well placed, as well as showing that they are breeding to a definite type. Their most satisfying moments to date must have been their win of Best of Breed at Crufts in 1995 with Ch. Beaulea Blue Print, who was also the top Miniature dog of that year, and having the top brood bitch in 1989 and 1990 with Jay Walker, and then again in 1995 with High Society. Also they took the top breeder award in 1996.

KADAMIN
Another who based her breeding foundation on the Iccabod lines is Karen Andres, who finished her first Champion, the home-bred Ch. Kadamin Miss Ribbons, in 1996. This is a daughter of Ch. Iccabod Travellers Tail who also carries Ch. Iccabod Mixed Herbs on her maternal pedigree, as well as being strong in Gildorwill breeding.

CASTILLA
Fred Morley and his late wife, Phyl, first became interested in Miniature Schnauzers back in the late sixties through the blacks, their first being a Ch. Jovinus Malya Swanee daughter who was, in fact, only the second black bitch to win a CC. Their first Champion was the pepper and salt Roundway-bred Ch. Castilla Galante who finished in 1969. He was the sire of their Ch. Dengarse Sue's Solitaire who was made up in 1973 and went on to be the top winning bitch of her era, with 17 CCs. Solitaire was bred by Mrs Hega Roberts out of the Canadian-bred Rosehill Bold Sue o'Handsworth.

The Morleys followed Sue's Solitare with another good bitch Champion, Castilla Zambra, a daughter of Ch. Iccabod Chervil and Castilla Golosina. She was to become the dam of the most famous Castilla, Ch. Linajudo, who certainly brought the breed right to the forefront with his Reserve Best in Show at Crufts in 1980, and then with his subsequent successes. He had first come to notice early, as an eight-months-old puppy at the South Wales Show, where he won the CC – another youngster with star potential spotted by the much-respected all-round judge, the late Bobby James. At his next show, on his home ground at Peterborough, Digby, as he was known, did even better, by taking Best of Breed and then the Utility Group, still as a puppy. Indeed, so successful was he as a puppy that he could not claim his crown until he won his sixth CC (and Best of Breed) – the first to be won after his first birthday; this was at Driffield in 1979 under Les Atkinson.

144

Ch. Castilla Linajudo (Ch. Fernery Fantastic ex Ch. Castilla Zambra). Bred & owned by Mr & Mrs Morley. The winner of 31 Challenge Certificates, was twice Best in Show at General Championship Shows and Reserve Best in Show at Crufts in 1980.
Photo: Anne Roslin-Williams.

In its heyday, the Contest of Champions was a prestigious charity gala event where the cream of British show dogs were invited to compete. The invitation was based on their successes at Championship shows through the previous year. It took the shape of a knockout contest with rounds being judged by different well-known judges. In 1980 Terry Thorn, Britain's Number One All-Rounder judge today, had the task of officiating for the final round of the Contest and he gave the nod to Ch. Linajudo, who could then truly be called a Champion of Champions. That Contest has now been rather overshadowed by the Pedigree Chum-sponsored Champion Finals, an annual highlight occasion where the winners of the prestigious and hotly contested Champion and Veteran Stakes held at Championship shows throughout the previous year compete in a grand finale.

Quickly following his success at the Contest, Linajudo won his Specialty Best in Show at the Schnauzer Club's Championship show, winning under the two Swedish judges, Marianne Frestadius and Benny Blid. Bath has often proved to be a good show for Miniatures over the years, and it was certainly the case for Linajudo in 1980 when he made a clean sweep against some of the country's top top competitors. Not only did he win the Champion Stakes overall under Bill Pinches, but he won the Group under Ben Johnson and Best in Show under Yvonne Bentinck. At his next show, Birmingham National, he also went Best in Show, having pleased Catherine Sutton in the Group and then Leslie Page for the Best in Show award. That year he was the nation's top winning

male of all breeds – a splendid end to a splendid year. In 1981 he repeated his Crufts breed win and enjoyed many other breed successes during the year. His final appearance was at Midland Counties where he won the Dog CC, his 31st and a breed record at the time.

Ch. Castilla Linajudo (the name means 'blue blood') won, overall, two Bests in Show, three Reserve Bests in Show and a Best Puppy in Show – all at general Championship shows. He won the Group nine times and was twice Runner Up. He won the Contest of Champions in 1989 and was a finalist in the Pedigree Chum Champion Stakes the next year. He also had a Specialty Best and qualified for his Junior Warrant. In all he won a total of 31 CCs (28 with BOB) along with 5 Reserve CCs. Home-bred, he was sired by Ch. Fernery Fantastic out of Ch. Castilla Zambra. Through his sire, he carried the Ch. Buffels All

American Boy of Deansgate, Ch. Risepark Toreador, Roundway Anklet and Settnor lines, while through his dam, a Ch. Iccabod Chervil daughter, he again tied in to the American-bred Ch. Risepark Bon Ell Taurus and Anklet lines. Through both his Champion offspring, his influence is carried on through the breed. The dog, Ch. Nosbod Daniel of Deansgate (the breed's first Pup of the Year finalist) sired the current record holder, Ch. Luke Lively. Daniel was bred by Mr and Mrs Dobson out of their first title-holder, Ch. Castilla Rea Quatro of Nosbod, a daughter of Ch. Catalanta True Luck at Risepark and Ch. Regalada in Castilla. Quatro was a good producer, with three Champions to her credit, the other two being sired by Ch. Deansgate Truey Nuff. Linajudo's Champion daughter, Ch. Castilla Odorifero, was out of Iccabod Time Traveller, bred from the two Travelmor imports US Mail and From US To You. Not only have the Morleys been very successful exhibitors with their Castillas, but even more importantly their bitches have proved excellent and prepotent producers, their blood being carried on by Champions and other good winners and producers throughout the breed. Of these, two of the most influential have to be the sisters, Ch. Real Quatro and Real Cinco, who produced five Champions between them to three different studs. Another is Linajudo's dam, Ch. Zambra, who also produced Ch. Castilla Diamante, owned by Pam Radford and Dorrie Clarke, when mated to the American-bred Ch. Irrenhaus Impact at Risepark. Diamante, the top winning Miniature of 1983 and a dual group winner, was mated to US Mail and produced three Iccabod Champions, while the fourth member of the litter, Iccabod Daydreamer at Risepark, was the dam of two Champions when mated to Impact.

In the first litter she produced the bitch Ch. Risepark Chase The Ribbons, and in her second and last litter she produced Ch. Irish Ch. Risepark Here Comes Charlie.

LEECURT

Ted and Sally Ilott, with the Leecurts, are involved in breeding all three colours of Miniature, and their lines are proving successful at all levels, with Best in Show

Ch. Leecurt Sweet Liberty (Spanish-bred Ch. Chipirrusquis Chipi at Kanix ex Leecurt Secret Dream). Bred by Mr & Mrs Ilott, owned by Mrs. Rogers. The first Leecurt Champion.

and Best Puppy in Show wins coming their way. The first title holder to carry the Leecurt affix was Rosemary Roger's pepper and salt bitch, who finished in 1992, Ch. Leecurt Sweet Liberty, a daughter of the Spanish-bred Ch. Chipirrusquis Chipi at Kanix and Leecurt Sweet Dream, herself a daughter of Ch. Iccabod Mixed Herbs.

AMURUS
Although they do not show their Miniatures nowadays, Pat Kidd and Marilyn Price enjoyed a most successful period showing their dogs during the late eighties and early nineties. In 1986, the year Pat's Ch. Dashing Dixie Dean – a US Mail son out of a Ch. Eastwight Sea Yank daughter – made his title, he also won the Group at Darlington under Joe Braddon and ended the year as the top winning Miniature. The following year, her Ch. Katar The Brothers Tale (also out of the same dam as Dixie Dean but by Ch. Iccabod Travellers Tail) won the Group under Jean Lanning, having won his first CC and BOB under Ferelith Somerfield. Soon after, at Richmond, he won his second ticket and was again Best of Breed under the great

American terrier expert, Ric Chashoudian.

The year 1988 was to prove a splendid year, with four youngsters from the litter by Ch. Dixie Dean out of Nosbod Maggie May making their successful debuts. Two of these gained their titles. Ch. Amurus Adorable Adora was campaigned by Pat Kidd, while the dog, Ch. Amurus Ansome Arry, was shown by Marilyn Price. Ch. Brothers Tale also finished his title that year. The following year, Ch. Maggie May (Ch. Fernery Fantastic ex Nosbod Gabrielle, a daughter of Ch. Deansgate Truey Nuff and Ch. Castilla Real Quatro) herself finished, just to show her children that anything they could do, she could do too! In the same year, Marilyn Price's Ch. Ansome Arry was the top winning Miniature in Britain.

TRAWEST
Trawest, the affix of Miss Pat Stewart, has been carried by a succession of both dogs and bitches who do well through puppyhood to maturity, particularly at the Open shows, where many Best Puppy and Best in Show awards come their way. Based on her imported bitch,

Ch. Amurus Ansome Arry (Ch. Dashing Dixie Dean ex Ch. Nosbod Maggie May). Bred by Mrs P. Kidd, owned by Miss M. Price. Born 1987, finished 1988, and first Champion for his owner.

Regency's Jana at Westra, and using the Iccabod males – in particular Ch. Iccabod Travellers Tail – she developed a recognisable stamp with her Miniatures.

The Irish show circuits were the scene for many of the early Trawest successes. In 1987 Trawest Almost American Mrs was the first Miniature to qualify for the Irish Pup of the Year contest. Trawest American Express was the first of three Trawests to make their Irish titles, being based on a points system, and going Best in Show at Killarney along the way. His litter brother, Joan and Cecil Williamson's Trawest American Reward, was Dog of the Year in Northern Ireland, despite not starting his campaign until the middle of the year.

The first British Champion was a daughter of Trawest Mainly American Mrs sired by Ch. Iccabod Travellers Tail, namely Ch. Trawest American Twist, who was made up in 1990. She was followed the next year by her younger sister when Ch. Trawest Nearly American Mrs gained her title (all very confusing, with so many "near Mrs"!), and she in turn was the dam of the latest to be made up by Miss Stewart, the male Ch. Trawest Nearly American Mr, a son of Ch. Iccabod Mixed Herbs. He finished in 1995.

ASHWICK
Pam and Dave Wick have enjoyed much success with their Miniatures but nowadays are less able to show and breed as much as they would perhaps wish. Their first Champion, made up in 1987, was the pepper and salt Ch. Deansgate Auntie Nuff of Ashwick, a daughter of Ch. Nosbod Gentleman Jack of Deansgate and Deansgate

Brighty Nuff. When mated to US Mail she produced Ch. Ashwick Bobbies Girl, the breed's top puppy in 1988 and the leading bitch the following year, and also Ch. Ashwick Mr Pickwick which they retained. He qualified for his Junior Warrant and made his title in 1990 before going to Anders Hanssen in Norway, where he not only became a National and International Champion and big-winning show dog, but also an important stud who had a strong influence on the Miniatures in Scandinavia. Another Ashwick who journeyed to Scandinavia was Ch. Ashwick Baby Love to Motown, who went to Pauline Bjorklund in Sweden, where she became a National and International Champion. The Wicks also sent a black and silver, Ashwick Silver Shadow, to Australia where he joined the highly successful Peppaz Miniatures of Betty Stothard and quickly became a Champion.

LICHSTONE
The Lichstone affix is shared by Stan Burke and his daughter, Mrs Ann McDermott, and her husband Tony, but with their breeding programme they are two separate lines. Over the years they have steadily bred both pepper and salt and black and silver, enjoying some nice wins along the way, especially at Open shows. The first Lichstone Champion was Chris Clay's Ch. Lichstone Country Maid, who finished in 1996. A Ch. Nortonchase Smart Alick daughter, she was bred by Stan Burke, who first became interested in the breed during the Deltone era, purchasing Ch. Deltone Deloklahoma towards the end of that dog's show career, and also owning the dual ticket winner, Deltone Delmemphis.

LEERICH

Jenny Richardson presents her dogs in good order and thoroughly enjoys showing them. Successful in Standards, with a home-bred Champion, she now also shows two home-bred Miniature bitches, Leerich Little Miss Piggy (co-owned with Jackie O'Dwyer), and Leerich Little Miss Fidget. Both are out of Rosavenda Dorocina, a daughter of Ch. Malenda Masterblend at Risepark. Miss Piggy is by the Spanish-bred Ch. Chipirrusquis Chipi at Kanix, while Miss Fidget is by Ch. Risepark Mister Nice Guy with Armorique. Both have now won their first CCs – Fidgit at the LKA in 1996, along with Best of Breed under Albert Wight, and Piggy at Bath 1997 from Jean Lanning.

BALMAR

The first Balmar Champion bred by Mrs Marjorie Bonnamy was Ch. Balmar Diamonda who was the result of Ch. Risepark Toreador mating her foundation bitch, Hemarco Crystal, a daughter of Ch. Buffels All American Boy of Deansgate. The second Champion was Carolyn Whitlock's (now Craig) Ch. Balmar Silver Cracker, out of Diamonda's litter sister and by Ch. Catalanta True Luck of Risepark. Another from the Crystal-Toreador mating was Rita and Charlie Baker's first Miniature Schnauzer, Balmar Saphette, who gave them their first Champion when she was mated to the Swedish-bred Ch. Jidjis Min Cato at Risepark, namely Ch. Leydean Sophie Serena, who finished in 1980.

All three of these Champions were good winners in the late seventies and early eighties, and, when Silver Cracker

Ch. Balmar Silver Cracker. Bred by Mrs M. Bonnamy, owned by Mrs C. Craig.

was mated to Glenys Allen's Ch. Malenda Mentha Mix, this gave Mrs Craig Ch. Malenda Mentha Santason, who won his title in 1992. He in turn is the sire of her current show dog, Ch. Gilberts Boy Wesleigh of Marbra, made-up in 1997. Santason was selected by Roger and Elaine Ward as the mate for their Ch. Wrendas Kristall Dream, the outcome being Mrs Viv Sanders' first title holder, Ch. Wrendas Dream Maker, who sired Ch. Zakmayo Billy Whizz, the top-winning Miniature Schnauzer for 1995.

Balmar Miss Blandish, a daughter of Ch. Chipirrusquis Chipi at Kanix, was exported to Denmark. Although not shown, she proved to be an excellent brood and is the dam of Norw. Swed.

Ch. Gillegoard Eye For Eye and also the littermates, Danish Ch. Gillegoard Intention, the top Miniature in Denmark for 1995, and her brother Danish Ch. Gillegoard Indy Car. In the UK, Charlie and Keith Yarnold's latest Daylorn to make its title is the Balmar Breakaway son, Ch. Daylorn Mister My Way, who is out of Daylorn Liberty Square, a US Mail and Ch. Castilla Odorifero daughter.

NOSBODS

Nowadays we do not see the Nosbods of June and Roy Dobson in the ring as much as in times gone by. However, they still produce a good one, either pepper and salt or black and silver, which is, perhaps, not surprising since their background goes back mainly to Castilla, Deansgate and Viento. Their Ch. Castilla Real Quatro at Nosbod was a good producing bitch with three Champions to her credit.

Interestingly, one of the breed's latest Champions, Pat and Harry Power's pepper and salt, Ch. Tilmondy Ace of the Peak at Sabrewood, who was made up in 1996, is a son of Nosbod Fun In the Dark. Ace made his title in three straight shows and finished in nineteen days – one of the quickest title runs ever.

MINIVALE

Carol and Terry Parnell's Minivale Talk Of the Town, as well as the black and silver bitch, Ch. Minivale Georgie Girl (sired by Ch. Arbey Ard T' Match) is also the dam of Ronnie Tierney's Ch. Minivale Professor Iggins at Nortonchase, who finished in 1996 and is yet another sired by Ch. Ringmaster. Mrs Tierney finished her first Champion,

the home-bred Ch. Nortonchase Smart Alick, a Ch. Katar The Brothers Tale son, in 1993.

CLARKMAR

Blacks were the initial interest of Wendy Clarke, but now she also breeds the pepper and salts. All her blacks stem from her imported black male, the American-bred Suelen Jet America, along with Rillaton breeding. Jet America is a son of Am. Ch. Suelen Frosty Brew and, through his dam, carries Am. Ch. Suelen Feldmar Snow Mobile and Am. Ch. Rampage's Waco Kid breeding. The pepper and salts have a mainly Eastwight foundation through her first Rownhams bitch, with the later addition of Ch. Malenda Masterblend at Risepark, introduced as an outcross sire. Recently Mrs Clarke imported the latest Travelmor to come to Britain – Travelmor's Proud To Be At Clarkmars (co-owned with Shaune Frost), who made his successful debut at the Miniature Club's Championship show under Sylvia Hammarstrom, who awarded him the Dog CC in 1996. He is a son of Am. Ch. Adamis Cocked and Reloaded and Travelmor Sparkling Wine, so through her he carries Am. Ch. Rampage's Express Mail and Am. Ch. Travelmors Champagne Lady.

DEANSGATE

Pamela McLaren and Elizabeth Cooke, Deansgate, have enjoyed several decades of success with their Miniatures since they made up Ch. Buffels All American Boy of Deansgate, their first Champion, in 1971. Some thirteen other British Champions have carried their affix, five of whom were campaigned by other exhibitors. They have also exported well over the years, with many Deansgates becoming Champions in their adopted homelands. The partners are renowned for their great sense of humour which is frequently reflected in their dogs' names – Hairs 'N' Graces, Ophelia Collar, Truey Nuff, Cor Tina, Fine Nance and the like.

One of the early outstanding show dogs bred by the partners was Ch. Deansgate Hairs 'N' Graces, owned by Anne-Thérèse Scott (now Mrs Scott-Abbott), handled by Geoff Corish, he was made up in 1975 and won a total of twelves CCs during his competitive years. He was the first Miniature to win a Utility Group, which he did at the Scottish Kennel Club in 1976. He was also Best in Show at the Miniature Club's Championship show in 1975 and was also the first of the breed to be invited to the Contest of Champions.

Dorothy Webster's Ch. Deansgate Truey Nuff, a Ch. Maximin Graben of Deansgate son, went best in show at Blackpool's 1983 Golden Jubilee Championship Show under Fred Dempster, when winning his first certificate, along with Best of Breed under Donald Becker and the Group under Hubert Arthur. In the same year Trueman won the Utility section of the sponsored New Faces Competition. He became a Champion the following year at Birmingham (National) under the late Joe Braddon.

The partners' Ch. Luke Lively at Deansgate, the breed's current record holder, enjoyed a splendid run of success from the middle eighties to the early nineties, during which time he amassed 40 CCs, the last being won at the LKA

Ch. Luke Lively at Deansgate (Ch. Nosbod Daniel of Deansgate ex Buryvale Time Lucky).
Bred by Misses Barlow & Halpern, owned by Misses McLaren & Cooke.
Top-winning Miniature of all time with 42 Challenge Certificates to his credit.
Photo: Pearce.

show in 1992 under Ellis Hulme. Luke is a son of the breed's first Pup of the Year finalist (in 1983), Ch. Nosbod Daniel of Deansgate and Buryvale Time Lucky, whose pedigree was a cocktail of Dengarse, Sonshea, Eastwight and Roundway, as well as tracing back to earlier Deansgate dogs including All American Boy. He was bred by the Misses Barlow and Halpern.

Although Luke never produced a British Champion, he had an extended show career with some exceedingly good wins, including his Best in Show at WELKS in 1988 under Leslie Page where he won the Group under Bob Flavell and the breed under Phyl Morley. Over the years he also did well in the sponsored Champion and Veteran Stakes, but never quite managed an overall win. He also enjoyed a remarkable level of success at the breed club Championship shows, going Best in Show at the Miniature Club's events in 1986, 1991 and 1992 and, on the two latter occasions, he won through from the Veteran class.

ARBEY
Betty and Archie Fletcher's first home-bred Champions were the littermates, Ch. Arbey Yankee Doodle and Ch. Arbey Yankee Starlet, both made up in 1977. They were out of their first Champion and foundation bitch, Ch. Short and Sweet at Deansgate, a daughter of Ch. Buffels All American

Boy of Deansgate, who had been mated to Ch. Eastwight Sea Yank to produce the Champion siblings. In a later litter to Ch. Eastwight Sea Goblin, Short and Sweet produced Ch. Arbey Penny Farthing, actually a male though his name might suggest otherwise. To date the Fletchers have made up sixteen Champions, with Ch. Arbey Yankee Starlet, Ch. Arbey Archer and Ch. Rimmick Ringmaster all going on to be top producers.

Mating their Champions Penny Farthing and Yankee Starlet together gave the Fletchers Ch. Arbey Shining Star. Starlet to Ch. Maximin Isbyorn produced Ch. Arbey Mistique. Isbyorn was interestingly bred, as his sire was Brynsmor Joker while his dam was the Swedish-titled but American-born Barclay Square Maximin Minx. From an Isbyorn daughter, Charnby Silver Dollar,

Ch. Rimmick Ringmaster (Eastwight Sea Master ex Rownhams Sea Fable). Bred by Mr & Mrs Smedley, owned by Mr & Mrs A. Fletcher. One of the breed's top sires.

Photo: Diane Pearce.

the Fletchers bred Ch. Arbey Sugar and Spice by the American-bred Skylines Leader at Rismount. The sister to Ch. Shining Star, Arbey Super Star, was mated to Brynsmor Mister Mischief, a dog who boasted the Swedish-bred Ch. Jidjis Min Cato at Risepark as his sire and the American-bred Maximin Minx as his dam. That resulted in Ch. Arbey Archer.

The two home-bred Champions, Archer and Sugar and Spice were bred together to produce Ch. Arbey Amber, while Ch. Adams Son at Arbey was bred by Janet Callow of the Buffels affix. His dam was the Arbey-sired Buffels Fancy Nancy, while his sire was Arbey Spice 'n' Sparks, a son of Ch. Sugar and Spice and Ch. Travelmors US Mail.

BUFFELS

When Janet Price, now Mrs Callow, returned home from America, after spending some years with Bill and Olive Moore and their Travelmor Miniatures, she brought with her Am. Ch. Travelmors Fantazio who carried Cosburns, Dorem and Benrook lines in his pedigree, and the bitch, Riversedge Petite Pebbles, who was mainly Geelong breeding. These two were mated together and produced Ch. Buffels All American Boy of Deansgate, owned by Pam Maclaren and Elizabeth Cooke. He played a prominent part in the breed's development through the seventies onwards, and was the breed's leading stud dog, with nine Champions, for nearly two decades. It was through his matings to Ch. Eastwight Sea Enchantment, which produced three Eastwight Champions, and to Fernery Honeysuckle, which produced Ch.

Fearnought of Fernery, the grandsire of Ch. Castilla Linajudo, that his influence on the breed has been strongest.

The partnership of Janet Callow and Betty and Archie Fletcher imported from Janice Rue in the USA the uncropped salt and pepper male, Suelen Rum Punch at Arbey and Buffels, and the cropped black and silver bitch, Suelen Ice Holiday. This brought in new blood and also gave the black and silver colour a boost, which has worked particularly well with their grandchildren when put to Ch. Rimmick Ringmaster.

ARBEYBUFFELS

As a result of breeding with these imports, Betty Fletcher and Janet Callow combined their affixes into Arbeybuffels and an interesting, and successful, line of Miniatures has developed carrying it. The Ringmaster son, Ch. Arbeybuffels This Guy Can, made up in 1993, was the first to carry the affix and he is now in New Zealand with Mike Brick, where he is one of the top winning Miniatures in that country. A younger brother, the black and silver Ch. Arbeybuffels Go North, made his title in four straight shows, a real achievement for the colour, and is the current most winning black and silver with seven CCs.

The partnership's Ch. Rimmick Ringmaster, with his combination of Eastwight Sea Master and Sea Gamble of Rownhams, gives a strong, almost exclusively, Eastwight background to his breeding. Bred by John Smedley, Ringmaster is a Group and multiple ticket winner, with sixteen CCs. He is also proving to be an outstanding sire with, currently, eight Champions to his credit. His daughter, Ch. Arbeybuffels

Miss Match Me, is the latest title maker for the partnership. She was Best in Show at the Miniature Club's 1996 Championship show under Sylvia Hammarstrom, owner of the Skansens Schnauzers in America, and was also the leading bitch and top puppy of that year.

WRENDRAS

Elaine and Roger Ward, with their Wrendras Miniatures, are also developing their own lines based on Iccabod, stemming from their foundation bitch, the Mixed Herbs daughter, Ch. Vandell Hazel Bee and her subsequent matings to Ch. Iccabod Travellers Tail. She was made up in 1989. Ch. Hazel Bee was bred by Daphne and David Snell, of the Vandell affix, and is a sister to Kevin and Jackie Durso's Ch. Vandell Apple Bee. Through their dam, Odalisque at Vandell, they carry the imported Skylines Leader of Rismount blood, and also trace back to Arbey and Risepark. The first title-holder to carry the Wrendras affix was Ch. Wrendras Kristall Dream, who was made up in 1991. A younger sister, Carol and Les Wareham's Ch. Wrendras Kristall Image, was made up in 1993.

Ch. Kristall Dream was duly mated to Carolyn Craig's Ch. Malenda Mentha Santason and this produced the dog, Ch. Wrendras Dream Maker, who was made up by Viv Sanders in 1995. He, in turn, sired the top winning Miniature of 1996, Ch. Zakmayo Billy Whizz, out of Wrendras Kristall Dawn, also owned by Mrs Sanders. Several Wrendras Miniatures have been exported and done well for their new owners. Wrendras Kristall Traveller went to Denmark and has, to date, sired three Champions there. In 1993 Ch. Vandell Hazel Bee was the top brood bitch and Wrendras also won the top breeders award. The Wrendras 'look' was perhaps epitomised with their success at Windsor when Ch. Hazel Bee and six of her progeny were the overall progeny class winners, this

Ch. Wrendras Kristal Dream and her sister Wrendras Kristal Blossom. Bred & owned by Mr & Mrs R. Ward. Photo: Alan V. Walker.

success having previously been enjoyed by the Eastwight kennel some years earlier.

JANSAD
Carol Daniels breeds both the pepper and salt and the black and silver and enjoys good wins in top company with both colours. Her first export, the black and silver male Jansad Steel Ice Man, who was the Best Puppy at the Miniature Club's Championship show in 1990 when Nils Jordal from Denmark judged, quickly became a National and International Champion in Europe. To date, Mrs Daniels has made up two Champions, both pepper and salt – the male, Ch. Rimmick Rival Bid at Jansad, in 1993 and the home-bred bitch, Ch. Jansad Ever So Evil, a Ch. Rimmick Ringmaster daughter, in 1994.

SILVERSOCKS AND APPLEWHITE
The partnership of Linda Forsyth and Kevin and Jacky Durso is developing a line with their Silversocks and Applewhite Miniatures, based on Ch. Vandell Apple Bee whom Kevin and Jacky made up in 1988, and Ch. Silversocks Made To Measure, made up by the partnership in 1992. Both are by Ch. Iccabod Mixed Herbs – with Made To Measure, through her Trawest dam, tracing back to Ch. Iccabod Travellers Tail and US Mail. The partnership also campaigned, to her Irish title, the bitch, Irish Ch. Silversocks Sensation, who is by Apple Bee out of Made To Measure. They also have an interest in the black colour and are currently successfully showing Clarkmars Crusader at Silversocks, bred by Mrs Wendy Clarke.

Space prevents my mentioning many of the enthusiastic breeders and exhibitors who have recently begun to contribute to the breed, but as it constantly attracts younger fanciers who are prepared to build on the foundations laid before, the breed seems to be in safe hands.

10 THE MINIATURE SCHNAUZER IN NORTH AMERICA

The Miniature Schnauzer of today owes much to the ever-growing influence of the American breeders, many of whose bloodlines are now spread throughout the world. Their influence in the Far East is especially strong at the present time. Dan Kiedrowski's bi-monthly publication *Schnauzer Shorts*, an ever-welcome arrival to breed enthusiasts in all parts of the world, is also a strong influence in promoting the American Miniatures.

With distance being a major factor for the American breeders and exhibitors, shows tend to be held in clusters and usually necessitate using a handler if one wishes to compete beyond regional level. Gaining the required number of points, including the necessary majors, to make a Champion can be an expensive exercise; and to campaign a Miniature (or any other breed) at the highest and most prestigious level to turn it into a top winner, involves much time and effort in travelling, as well as financial outlay.

At the highly regarded national and regional specialities, Miniatures more often than not have a numerically good and representative entry, which is especially so for the Montgomery County KC weekend cluster of shows which includes the American Miniature Schnauzer Club annual National Specialty. This event is held in early October, and the ever-growing following of overseas enthusiasts who attend, as well as the actual Miniatures in competition, make it the highlight series of shows of the year. This one weekend is certainly one of the few times in the year when many of America and Canada's top terriers vie with one another for the breed and Group honours.

The American Miniature Schnauzer Club holds three Specialties a year, which are held in conjunction with the Chicago International Show in April, the Great Western in June and Montgomery County in October.

The judges for both the regular classes and the sweeps at these events are selected first by nomination, then ten are voted on by the entire club membership, with those receiving the most votes being allowed to select which of the three shows they would like to judge – understandably most choose Montgomery County. There must be a five-year gap before a name can come up for re-nomination. There are around twenty-three local Miniature Schnauzer Clubs that also hold a Specialty show during the year, with some six of them staging two. The selection of judges for all these is done in a variety of ways.

DISTURBING TRENDS
In recent years the American Miniatures appear to be moving away from the true sturdy Schnauzer type of past years, and a leggier, more narrow, decidedly upright, more terrier-looking Miniature appears to be gaining favour with a growing number of judges; sadly these also include breed specialists. Colouring, too, is a cause for concern. The pepper and salt, with its individually banded hair colour, is unique to the Schnauzer family, and this ranges, in individual dogs and bitches, from an even, light pewter silver-grey through to a dark steel colour.

Unfortunately this is being diluted through the regular and continual mixing of the three colours, the banding with the individual hairs is being lost and, once gone, it will have disappeared for ever. With the blacks and black and silvers, we also see colour deterioration through this mixing. On the Continent mixing the colours is not permitted except in special circumstances, and when done it is strictly regulated.

ESTABLISHING THE MINIATURE SCHNAUZER
It was in 1927 at the Combined Terrier Show that Miniatures first had separate classes, although it was not until some six years later that both breeds were actually to have separate classifications. The American Miniature Schnauzer Club was formed (as was the Standard Schnauzer Club of America) in 1933 when the American Kennel Club decreed that a speciality club could only sponsor one breed. Miniatures first arrived in America from the early twenties, with something over one hundred being imported during the first ten years, the majority of them from Germany, although almost all of these dogs were to have little or no part in the modern-day Miniatures' background.

MARIENHOF
It was four dogs sent over to Mrs Marie Slattery in 1924, Amsel v. d. Cyriaksburg and her two daughters, Lotte and Lady

Am. Champion Kelly's Pebwin's Hallelujah. Hal is the top-producing black sire, with 23 American Champions and also a Best in Show winner. Photo: The Standard Image.

v. d. Goldbachohe, along with the male, Mack v. d. Goldbachohe, that were to form the true beginnings of the American-bred Miniature Schnauzers, as well as the foundation for Mrs Slattery's Marienhof kennels, from which more than one hundred Champions would emerge, during nearly fifty years of her devoted involvement with the breed.

Later, in 1927, she imported the mature male Cuno v. Burgstadt as a replacement after Mack's untimely death. Cuno was to become the most influential of all the imported males, despite being mainly used only by Mrs Slattery on Amsel and her daughters before he was tragically killed and his true value was realised. Another import, who was also a Cuno son, Marko v. Beautenberg, was to prove yet another important stud for Mrs Slattery, as did his grandson, Am. Ch. TMG of Marienhof. The first American-bred Miniature to finish, Moses Taylor of Marienhof, was bred by Marie Slattery.

LEDAHOF
Leda Martin, another pioneer breeder with the Ledahof Miniatures, was responsible for importing another influential male in Flieger Heinzelmännchen, and he and the progeny of Cuno were to blend well over these two early decades, with the breed, in essence, then developing through their lines.

IMPORTANT BROTHERS
The three brothers, Sandmann, Stylobate and Cockerel of Sharvogue, also had an early influence on the breed through their progeny – especially Stylobate, who was felt by many fanciers to be the best of the trio. A daughter of his, Ch. Dorem Searchlight, was the dam of Ch. Dorem Display, thus making Stylobate a significant influence.

The brothers produced well, over the years, but, sadly, Stylobate had little opportunity to establish himself. He was owned as a pet and then was accidentally killed as a very young dog, shortly after going Best of Breed at Westminster in 1941. Nevertheless, he did sire four Champions and four top producers from four different bitches.

DOREM
Miss Dorothy Williams with the Dorem Miniatures was another enthusiast dedicated to the breed, with over forty home-bred Champions to her credit, including the great Ch. Dorem Display, who was born in April 1945 and later owned by Mrs Meldon, who campaigned him extensively.

"Display's influence on the American Miniatures can be considered nothing short of phenomenal, both as a show dog and sire" – to quote Dan Kiedrowski in *The New Miniature Schnauzer*. As a show dog he was the first Miniature Schnauzer to win Best in Show, which he did in 1946. The next year he won the Group at Westminster, again the first Miniature to do so. He also enjoyed four Specialty Bests.

Display was whelped at the end of the war, at a time when interest in breeding and showing was growing in popularity. He also represented a more stylish and smarter type of Miniature, which pleased in the Group and Best in Show competitions. He was also widely campaigned, bringing the breed to the notice of a wider public, to whom it was until then little known. As a sire, Display's influence was total and complete, dominating succeeding generations in the breed through top-producing and influential sons and daughters.

Display was only ten months old when his first Champion son, Ch. Dorem High Test, was whelped, to be quickly followed by Ch. Dorem Tribute and the litter brothers, Ch. Diplomat and Ch. Delegate of Ledahof, who were all born in that same year, thus quickly establishing Display's reputation as a successful sire – and all while he himself was still making his big wins.

Am. Ch. Sibehill's Dark Shadows.
An outstanding black, and top Miniature
1986 & 1987. *Handled by Joan Huber.*
Photo: Fox & Cook.

PHIL-MAR

His litter sister, Ch. Dorem Shady Lady, the matriarch for Mrs Peggy Anspach Wolfe, also proved outstanding. As a producer, she was to influence succeeding generations of Phil-Mar Miniatures. Her three Champion daughters, Ch. Phil-Mar Watta Lady, Ch. Phil-Mar Gay Lady and Ch. Phil-Mar Lucky Lady, were all top producers. A grandson, Ch. Phil-Mar Lugar, proved to be both an outstanding show dog and and outstanding sire. He was twice a Best in Show winner and he sired twenty-six Champions, including the top-producing Ch. Blythewood Main Gazebo, with thirty-one Champions to his credit.

BLYTHEWOOD

From the early trend-setting days, there has been a steady flow of outstanding dogs and bitches that have influenced the breed and made their mark over the years. The Blythewoods of Joan Huber are such Miniatures. They have been consistently and extremely successful since their beginnings in the fifties when the first home-bred Champion, Blythewood Merry Melody, was finished.

Joan Huber has proved successful over the years both as a breeder, having produced upwards of two hundred Champions, and as a professional handler, with several of her charges occupying the number one spot in the breed in various years – the first was her own Ch. Blythewood Chief Bosun in 1966, the black Ch. Sibehills Dark Shadows in 1986and 1987, and others right into the present.

The Blythewoods have also been exported to all corners of the globe, where they have not only been the foundation for many successful kennels, but have also played their part in the progress and development of the breed in the lands of their adoption.

Over the decades there have been many outstanding and top-producing studs. The Best in Show and multi-

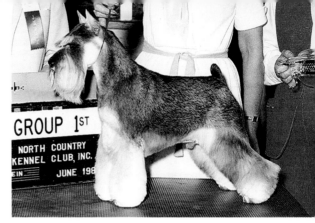

Am. Ch. Blythewood National Acclaim
Both an outstanding show dog, plus 32
Champions to his credit.
Photo: Kiedrowski.

Am. Ch. Blythewood Shooting Sparks.
Bred & owned by Joan Huber.
The top, living sire with 57 AKC
Champions and, to date, the kennel's most
successful homebred sire.   Photo: Klein.

Specialty winner Ch. Blythewood
Shooting Sparks (Am. Can. Ch.
Blythewood My Best Shot ex Ch.
Blythewood She's A Fox) is the breed's
top living sire, with fifty-seven
Champions to date to his credit.

   To quote Dan Kiedrowski: 'Joan
Huber is a past master in the art of
grooming and presentation, with all her
charges having a style, balance and
smartness that is instantly recognisable.
She stresses the importance of appreci-
ating each animal's individual structure,
and then gives attention to detail as well
as having an eye for line and form.'

SKYLINE'S
Skyline's, the Miniature Schnauzers bred
by Carol Parker, enjoyed many

outstanding successes during the
seventies and eighties. The first
Champion she bred was Ch. Skylines
Silver Lining, a daughter of Ch. Laddin
of Arador and Ch. Orbits Lift Off. She,
in turn, produced six Champions, five of
which, like their dam, also became
multiple Champion producers.

   Her most famous son was Ch.
Skyline's Blue Spruce, sired by Ch.
Skyrockets Upswing. His potential was
quickly recognised for, on his show
debut at just one day over six months of
age, he took the Best of Breed, with his
title quickly following. While making his
title he enjoyed four Sweepstake Bests
and two Best of Winners at Specialties,
including Montgomery County in 1974,
where he also went Best of Breed the

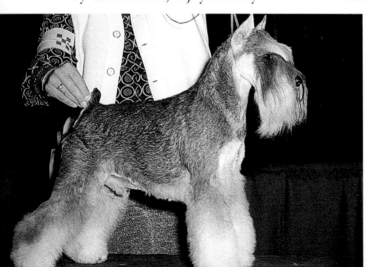

Am. Ch. Skyline's Blue
Spruce.
Bred & owned by Carol
Parker, he is one of the
breed's all-time top
winners and producers.

Photo: Roberts.

following year under Olive Moore.

Blue Spruce enjoyed six Specialty Bests during his show career and was the top Miniature (Knight system) in 1976. He, too, was a dog whose potential as a sire was recognised early, particularly as his son from his first litter, Ch. Skyline's Star Spangled Banner, was his closest competitor in 1976 and this son of Ch. Skyline's Little Britches (also a Silver Lining daughter) followed his sire as the Top Miniature in 1977. Banner proved to be an all breeds Best in Show winner and also had ten Specialty Bests to his credit. Banner's sister, Ch. Skyline's Fern of Winrush also produced well, being the dam of three Champions.

Carol Parker purchased Ch. Valharras Extra Allaruth as an outcross after he had made his title in 1981 and he was campaigned by Clay Coady, tying as the breed winner in 1982. The following year Carol Parker was to enjoy yet another breed number one (Knight system), this time with another outstanding home-bred male, namely Ch. Skyline's Storm Signal. He epitomised much of what Mrs Parker felt was true Miniature Schnauzer type. Signal was the first Miniature to take Best of Breed on the four consecutive days of the Montgomery County weekend and this he did in 1983. He went Best at Montgomery again the following year and also won three Specialties in a row.

IRRENHAUS

Jacqueline Hicks, with the Irrenhaus Miniatures, was another breeder who produced a strongly recognisable type that continued on through the generations and years, as well as through

Am. Ch. Irrenhaus Blueprint.
Bred & owned by Jackie Hicks.
Sire of 19 American Champions and a
cornerstone sire.   Photo: John L. Ashbey.

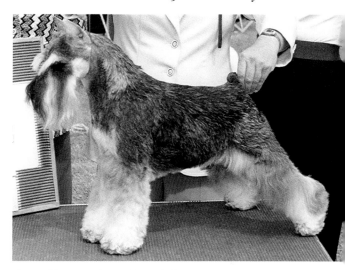

Am. Ch. Irrenhaus Stand Out.
Bred & owned by Jackie Hicks, handled by
Sue Baines.
A Best in Show winner and the sire of 21
American Champions.   Photo: Bushman.

several outstanding winners and producers.

The Specialty and Group winning Ch. Irrenhaus Flights of Fancy (a Blue Spruce daughter) was the top bitch in 1978 and also set a breed record with her all-Champion litter of six, sired by

Ch. Imperial Stamp O'Kharasahl. To Ch. Kharasahl Blue Chips, another Blueprint son, she produced two further title-makers. Her litter brother, Ch. Irrenhaus Blue Print, proved an outstanding sire with upwards of twenty Champions to his credit. He too was a Group and Specialty winner.

The Number One Miniature Schnauzer (Knight system) for 1984 was Ch. Irrenhaus Survivor, a son of the Best in Show-winning Ch. Irrenhaus Stand Out – aptly named, for, as one of that all-Champion litter, he was not only a top winner but sired over twenty Champions. Among Survivor's sixteen Champions was Ch. Irrrenhaus Classic who, in turn, sired Ch. Gough's Class Act O'Pickwick, the No. 1 Miniature Schnauzer (all systems) for 1995 and 1996. Survivor's dam, Ch. Irrenhaus Bluet, in her litter to the 1980 Montgomery winner, Ch. Irrenhaus Stamp of Approval, produced Eng. Ch. Irrenhaus Impact at Risepark, who was sent over to England, where he lived up to his name both as a sire, with eleven Champions to his credit out of bitches with varying backgrounds, and as a show dog, where his successes included a Specialty Best during a relatively short show career.

REGENCY

The Regency story really begins with the Ch. Marchiem Poppin Fresh daughter, Jana P.D., which Beverly Verna had purchased in the middle seventies with the intention of mating her to the record-setting Ch. Hughcrest Hugh Hefner, the famous son of Poppin Fresh. But that proved to be too complicated for a beginner so, instead, she was bred to the young local dog, Ch. Skylines Blue Spruce, who was just beginning his Specials career. The outcome, as they say, is history. This mating was repeated twice more and, in total, produced seven Champions, with two proving to be very special. From the first mating came the male, Ch. Regency's Right On, and from the second came the bitch Ch. Regency Rosy Glow. Their sister, Ch. Regency's Reward, was also to prove a top producer.

The male was the first Regency to enjoy a Specials career, winning many Best of Breed. He also sired thirty-seven Champions and proved to be Blue Spruce's top-producing son, while the bitch Rosy Glow is, Bev feels, one of the best bitches she has ever handled but, although Rosy Glow won two Groups, she did not achieve her potential – the time was not right to special a bitch.

Who to mate Rosy to, with her outcross pedigree, was the subject of much discussion and debate between Bev, Dan Kiedrowski and Carol Parker (Skyline), and the outcome was that her

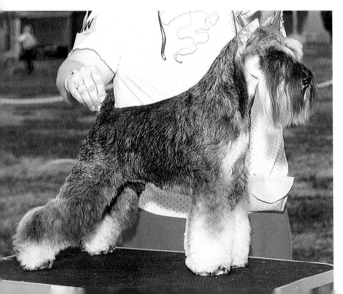

Am. Ch. Regency's Right On Target.
Bred & owned by Bev Verna.
The top-producing Miniature of all time, Target sired an amazing 78 American Champions, with more abroad.

Photo: MikRon.

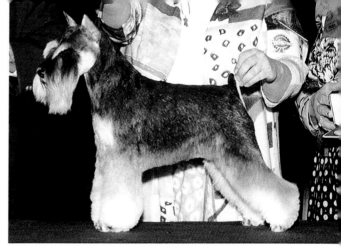

Am. Ch. Das Feder's Drivin' Miss Daisy, an outstanding bitch and the Number One Miniature for 1994, handled by Bev Verna. Booth Photography.

full brother, Right On, was chosen – a carefully calculated decision. From that mating came four puppies, with one, a male, proving outstanding right from the very first. Bev recalls that he was the one you just could not take your eyes off and, as he grew, he always retained his early promise and style, always looking completely balanced and "right", and so he was named Right On Target.

Always shown in the bred-by-exhibitor class, Target finished his Championship at nine months of age, with a National Specialty win and then, a week later, going Group One at the prestigious Golden Gate show. During his show career he enjoyed many Bests of Breed, Group wins (eleven) and Group placements, along with seven Specialty bests and an all breed Best in Show. In 1982 he tied for the breed's number one spot.

It was as a sire that Target contributed to the breed and, like his grandsire Blue Spruce, he was to prove a great one and his influence, too, was to be instant and dramatic. He set a new one-year producing record in 1984 with nineteen Champions, repeating this in 1985, and he went on to lead all sires for the next three years, with his progeny not only proving outstanding in the show ring but also as producers. His seventy-eight Champion offspring makes him the top-producing Miniature of all time. Only nine of these offspring carry the Regency affix, as his success was not dependent on any one kennel – a fact that gives Bev Verna much gratification.

Although Target was Regency's proudest accomplishment, there have been others. One was the cleverly-named Ch. Regency Equal Rights, a Right On daughter who, when she finished, was the first *uncropped* Miniature to become an American Champion for forty-eight years.

Bev Verna handled the black Target son, Judy and Bill Sousa's Ch. Regency Shot in the Dark, the first of his colour to achieve the breed number one spot, which he did in 1985. The year before that he had also been the first black to win an AMSC Sweeps, which he won under Sue Baines (Irrenhaus).

Interestingly the black Target daughter, Ch. Jubilees Jokers Wild, also owned by the Sousas, was the top winning bitch for 1988 and 1989.

Another high-spot achievement was with the Target grand-daughter, Ch. Das Feder's Drivin' Miss Daisy, a daughter of Ch. Jerry O'S Sharpshooter O'Daree and Ch. Repetitions P.B. Productions, owned by Larry and Georgina Drivon. Daisy was the number one Miniature in 1994 and, in achieving this, she did the most winning in one year achieved by a bitch, which included two Bests in Show all breeds, fifteen Group first and twenty-four additional placings, along with eleven Specialty bests.

*Am. Ch. Allaruth's Charles v. Sole Baye.
An outstanding son of Ch. Sole Baye's T.J.
Esquire, his wins included fifteen Specialty
bests. Now proving himself a producing
sire.* *Photo: Holloway.*

SOLE BAYE

Yvonne Phelps, with the Sole Baye
Miniatures, began her interest in the
breed back in the early sixties and, as
with so many people, it all started
through her first Miniature – a pet, who
was Hilda v. A transforming grooming
session and a first-ever visit to a local dog
show proved the spur – "to breed a
Champion".

Hilda had an interesting background
on both sides of her pedigree and this,
along with the guidance and support of
Gloria Weidlein (of Landmark fame) in
the early years, set "Billie", as Yvonne is

known, on the road to success. Since
those early years there have been some
really outstanding winners and producers
to carry the affix both in America and
abroad. The Sole Baye affix comes from
Billie's English origins and home-town –
a charming small East Coast Suffolk
seaside town – while most of the dogs
are named after famous racehorses.

For Hilda's second litter, Ch.
Landmark's Masterpiece was selected as
the sire, and from this mating came two
Champions, with the bitch, Ch. Sisterce
of Sole Baye, being retained. She was
mated to Fanciways Daktari and this
produced Ch. Manta of Sole Baye who,
in turn, produced Ch. Sole Baye's Miss
Musket, the first top-producer for the
kennel, with seven Champions. The
most famous of these was Ch. Sole
Baye's Sundowner (by Ch. Sunshine
Sounder), a multiple Specialty winner
with a host of Group placements.

Miss Musket, for her fourth and final
litter, was mated to Ch. Tomei Super
Star and from this came Ch. Sole Baye's
John Henry and Ch. Sole Baye's
Tamure, both of whom were to play an
important part in the ongoing Sole Baye
successes.

John Henry joined Angel Pons in
Spain, where he not only became a
national and international Champion
but, more importantly, played his part in
the breed's development in Europe
through the use of American breeding
there. Before he left for his new home he
had sired some outstanding stock,
among whom was Ch. Sole Baye's T.J.
Esquire, to date the sire of 26 AKC
Champions and eight Champions
overseas. John Henry also won six
Specialty Bests, his last at six years of

Am. Ch. Rampage's Express Mail.
Bred & owned by Janice Ramel, handled
by Carol Garmaker.
Proving to be an influential sire both in
North America and overseas, with 36
AKC Champions to date.
Photo: Bill Francis Photography

age, and in 1995 he made his final appearance at the AMSC Specialty in conjunction with the Great Western weekend, winning the Veteran Stakes.

He sired Ch. Allaruths Charles v. Sole Baye, bred by Ruth Ziegler, and shown by Maripi Wooldridge. His career encompassed winning fourteen Specialties (including three of the parent club), multiple Group firsts and placements, as well as Best of Breed at Westminster in 1990 and 1991. He was the No. 2 Miniature for three consecutive years. To date Charles has sired sixteen Champions, seven of which are out of Ch. Sole Baye's Winning Colours, the top-producing daughter of T.J. Esquire and a granddaughter of Ch. Sole Baye's Tamure.

One of this combination, Ch. Sole Baye's Johnar, co-owned with Sawako Oba, made a piece of breed history at Evansville KC in March 1997 by going Best in Show under Mrs B. Stenmark in the highest overall entry ever (over 4,000) when a Miniature Schnauzer has won the premier award. Another Charles son, Am. Argentinian Ch. Sole Baye's Broadside, is a Best in Show and multiple Specialty winner and also the current Number One Schnauzer (all sizes) in Argentina.

The decades have certainly shown that Billie Phelps has bred her Sole Baye Champions – the record shows that there have been outstanding ones that have also been top producers.

BANDSMAN
Carole Weinberger with the Bandsman Miniatures has been involved with the breed for some twenty-five years now, and encapsulates her conception of the

breed thus: "The Miniature Schnauzer as a small working dog has formed the basis of my thinking and breeding programme" – a belief reinforced over the years by her travels and friendships with other breeders committed to the Miniature Schnauzer from around the world. Only in the United States and Canada is the Miniature shown in the Terrier Group.

Ch. Repetitions Renaissance, a Ch. Skyrockets Upswing daughter, was the real foundation of Carole's kennel. Poppy, as she was called, had a very good Specials career, winning twenty-six Bests of Breed in the strong competition of the day as well as numerous Group placements, with only limited showing covering just two years.

Poppy also proved to be an excellent producer, with outstanding Champions to her credit. In her litter to Ch. R-Bo's Victory Flash, himself the sire of thirty Champions, came her best-producing

Am. Ch. Rampage's Representative (Am. Ch. Rampage's Express Mail ex Am. Ch. Repetitions Positive Attitude).
Bred by Carol Garmaker & Janice Rammel, owned by Mrs Garmaker, Mrs Rammel and Mr & Mrs Hal Smith.
'Rep' is simply the top-winning Miniature Schnauzer in breed history and proving an equally outstanding cornerstone sire.
Photo: Booth.

daughter, Ch. Bandsman's Bouquet. From Bouquet's first litter – a mating to Ch. Irrenhaus Sensation – all four pups went on to become Champions and top producers and all finished on or before their first birthday. The dog was Ch. Bandsman Talisman and the three bitches were Ch. Bandsman Free Spirit, Ch. Bandsman Cookie Bouquet and Ch. Bandsman Postscript, the latter being the successful foundation for the Postscript kennels, joining them as a four-months-old puppy. Handled by Sue Baines she went on to become the top bitch, all systems, of 1986.

Am. Can. Ch. Bandsman Free Spirit (Clover) also proved to be a particularly good producer, with eleven out of seventeen of her puppies finishing, several of whom went on to have fine show records with Group and Specialty wins, and her line continues at Bandsman.

A particularly memorable win for Carole was taking the Points at Montgomery County with the Clover grand-daughter Ch. Bandsman They Broke the Mold from the puppy class. Interestingly, four times during the eighties, the Montgomery County Sweeps, or best opposite winners were

Bandsman dogs, and all of them were Renaissance grandchildren or great-grandchildren.

A litter bred in 1984 by Jerry Oldham of Jerry O's interested Carole and, as a result, Ch. Jerry O's Future Shock, a dark pepper and salt bitch who carried the black and silver gene, joined Bandsman and, when shown, she finished faster than any dog or bitch Carole has ever owned before or since. She was in the puppy class twice, winning both days, and then shown five times in the Open, going Winners Bitch or better at each show, finishing up with four majors and two Best of Breed, along with two Group placements.

As a brood bitch she produced four significant Champions, each special in its own way, with the most significant mating by far being to her half-brother by Ch. Rampages Waco Kid – the black and silver dog Ch. Jerry O's Raincheck. From this mating came Ch. Bandsman Newsprint ('Scoop'). Although not specialed a great deal, his qualities, especially his dazzling black colour, good dark eye, superb topline and set-on, as well as his ground-covering movement, were all appreciated by other serious breeders and, as a result, many quality bitches were sent to him, resulting in some twenty-nine Champions to date, with many others pointed. He is currently the all-time top-producing black and silver male, displacing his famous grandsire, Waco Kid, who had led the score with twenty-five Champions. Sadly, a back injury is taking its toll on 'Scoop', limiting his stud career.

With this in mind, Carole began to think of the need for another black and silver male and so bred the very sound black and silver-carrier bitch, Ch. Always Room for Jello, a Newsprint grand-daughter, to Ch. Adamis State Of The Art, who combined the look of his sire, Ch. Rampages Express Mail, with Irrenhaus. From the mating the lone black and silver in the litter just filled the eye right from the very first, and he has become Ch. Bandsman's Why Not, a Group and Specialty winner.

With two Champions already, this early in his stud career, the combination of the Newsprint offspring to Why Not, and vice versa, works extremely well, and with the choice of the Adamis dog proving to have been a good one, the future looks full of promise for the continuing progress of the Bandsman breeding programme.

TRAVELMOR

Travelmor has enjoyed successes that extend over some four decades now. Their dogs have always been a hobby and nearly always owner-handled in the early years, firstly with Bill and Olive Moore at the helm and nowadays with their daughter, Jenny. Their successes have included many prestigious Specialty and Sweep wins over the years.

The home-bred Ch. Travelmor's

Witchcraft was an early example of their breeding and success. He enjoyed some sixty-four Bests of Breed, going on to nearly half that number of Group placements. He sired five Champions, with Ch. Travelmor's Fantzio going to England in the late sixties, where, along with his son, Ch. Buffels All American Boy of Deansgate, he played a significant part in the breed's progress there.

In the early eighties two cleverly named Travelmors, the bitch, Travelmor's From Us To You, and the dog, Travelmor's US Mail, also went over to England to join Pam Radford and Dorrie Clarke with the well-known Iccabod Miniatures, the bitch going first. Both were out of Ch. Reflections Lively Image, a paternal Ch. Penlan Peter Gunn daughter, and maternal Ch. Skyrockets Uproar grand-daughter. The bitch had Ch. Skyrockets Travel More as her sire and the dog had Ch. Skylines Blue Spruce as his. Both had a spectacular show career and also proved themselves as producers, each having a significant influence on the breed. US Mail is the breed's current top stud in Britain, with 17 Champions.

They easily made their titles and both were Best in Show winners at a British general all-breed Championship show – with the overall entry at such events usually being well over the ten thousand mark. Both were also Specialty winners, the dog winning at both the Schnauzer Club's event for all sizes of Schnauzer, and the Miniature Club's Silver Jubilee show in 1984.

Yet another male from Travelmor has been sent over to England, Travelmor Proud To Be At Clarkmars, and he joined Wendy Clarke (Clarkmars) and

Shaune Frost (Armorique) in 1996. This son of Ch. Adamis Cocked And Reloaded, out of the Ch. Rampages Express Mail daughter Travelmor Sparkling Wine, made his show debut at the Miniature Club's Specialty, where he was the Best Puppy and also won the Challenge Certificate for dogs under Sylvia Hammarstrom, owner of the well-known Skansen Giant Schnauzers in California.

On the home front, Ollie and Jenny have widened their breeding base of late with the introduction of such outstanding and dominant studs as Ch. Rampages Express Mail and Ch. Allaruth Charles v. Sole Baye, together with Ch. Adamis Cocked and Reloaded and his maternal grandsire, Ch. Adamis State of the Art. Emphasis with the bitches centres on Ch. Travelmor's Champagne Lady (by Ch. Travelmor Triumph out of a Bound to Win – Lively Image daughter), and her non-Champion daughter Sophisticated Lady (by Charles) along with her three daughters, two sired by Ch. Jerry O's Sharp Shooter O'Daree. All these dogs hold the key to the future for Travelmor.

PENLAN

Having been influenced by seeing Ch. Yankee Pride Colonel Stump at Westminster back in 1959 on their first-ever visit to a dog show, Landis and Penny Hirstein determined to own a Miniature and, like many, although well-intentioned, they started with one that did not make the grade.

Despite inevitable early set-backs and disappointments, they persevered, and with a lot of enthusiasm and hard work that has continued over the decades,

they have developed the Penlan dogs and bloodlines to be among the most respected and admired in the breed, a respect and regard that extends worldwide.

It is said that third time is lucky and, for the Hirsteins, so it proved, as their third foundation bitch was Hellary's Lolly, a significant daughter of Dorem Corsair and also a half-sister to the dam of Ch. Hellary's Dark Victory, a dog they much admired at the time, who also had an attitude that said "I own the ring."

From her first litter, when she was mated to Ch. Hellary's Danny Boy, Dark Victory's younger brother, Lolly produced Penlan Cadet Too, an exaggerated bitch in many ways but with much quality and breed type, which she passed on to all of her puppies. She was also a tightly line-bred bitch, carrying many top-producing dogs and bitches in her pedigree. So, with this tightly-bred background and the careful selection of her mates who were each selected for specific reasons, a very strong line of bitches was developed that contributed much to the successes that the Hirsteins were to enjoy over the succeeding years, both as exhibitors and breeders. Cadet is not only the Hirsteins' top-producing bitch to date, with ten Champions to her credit, but she was also a very special Miniature as a family pet and companion. All the Penlans trace back to her and her dam.

Her most significant son was Ch. Penlan Paragon who was also the kennel's first Group winner. He came from Cadet's third litter, which was to Ch. Phil Mar Dark Knight and was to prove the sire of eleven Champions– all from Penlan bitches – among whom was Ch. Penlan Paragon's Pride, another outstanding stud who produced some thirty title-makers, many to outside kennels, as he proved to be a popular stud both for his looks and also his producing pedigree. He in turn was to sire Ch. Penlan Paperboy, another top producer with forty-four Champions.

When Cadet was mated to Ch. Hellary's Dark Victory she produced only one puppy. This was Ch. Penlan Prelude To Victory. She proved an outstanding winner and was also the Hirsteins' first Montgomery winner. As a producer she, too, was significant, and also the grand-dam of Ch. Penlan Peter Gunn, one of the breed's all-time greats both as a spectacular show dog and as a record-making sire, with seventy-three Champions that included four top-producing sons. He was also the breed's top sire in his own lifetime.

Peter Gunn was sold as a young Champion to Dr and Mrs Beiles (Carolane) and handled throughout his career by Claudia Seaberg. He set many breed firsts, with some outstanding Specialty bests and Group wins and placements, as well as Best in Show wins. He was the number one in 1977.

Dick and Joanne Trubee, professional handlers who specialised in Miniature Schnauzers, not only handled the early Penlan Champions but also became very good and helpful friends. This association lasted until the premature death of Dick and the retirement of Joanne, when the Hirsteins began to handle other people's dogs as well as their own, and then to handle the puppies they sold – and then their puppies later. They branched out into

Am. Ch. Penlan Polarity.
One of the many outstanding Penlan Miniatures, bred & shown by Landis & Penny Hirstein.   *Photo: Booth.*

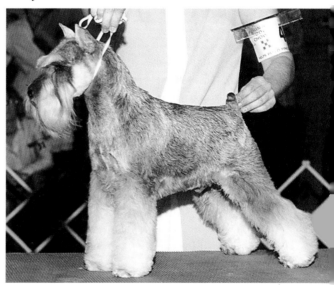

Am. Ch. Penlan Peter Gunn.
Bred & owned by Landis & Penny Hirstein. The record-breaking sire of 73 American Champions.   Photo: Twomey.

other bloodlines and breeds, campaigning some outstanding dogs and bitches.

Over the years those dogs they have handled and Penlan-bred dogs and bitches have consistently made the top ten rankings in the breed as well as enjoying the number one spot with Ch. Cyngars Ultimatum (a Paperboy son) in 1978 and Ch. Bardon Bounty Hunter (a Ch. Penlan Checkmate son) in 1980. They have also bred five all breed Best in Show winners and they take particular pride in the fact that Ch. Penlan Promissory won two of his four bests from the classes. He was also a multiple Specialty winner and went on to become a fourth generation Penlan top-producing sire.

As Dan Kiedrowski states in his *The New Miniature Schnauzer*, "Penlan since its inception has bred more top producers than any other kennel before or since." Eleven sires of five or more Champions and sixteen dams of three or more Champions carry the Penlan affix and all are descended from Hellary's Lolly. More important, perhaps, is that the Hirsteins have always been happy to share with others their wealth of experience

SERCATEP
Although Debbie and Del Herrell's first Miniature was a Champion-sired pepper and salt and purchased in 1974, a year later they discovered the black and silver colour and since those days their interest has centred on the colour, and over the years the Sercateps have played their part in the black and silver's progress.

Their first black and silver was purchased at eight months of age and he became Champion Tammashann's Town Strutter, their first Champion. In those days he was usually the only black and silver in competition against many pepper and salts and a few blacks. Their next major purchase was Ch. Glory's

Eager Beaver, who had already made his title at just over one year of age. His pedigree combined perfectly with their own line, going to similar breeding of Ch. Landmarks Masterpiece. Eager Beaver was needed to improve rear movement and shorten backs, and, although a pepper and salt, his black and silver puppies had excellent black hard coats and better rears.

The combination of Town Strutter daughters bred to Eager Beaver gave both their first top winner and also their first top producer. Ch. Sercateps Midnite Memory earned top black and silver bitch status with her Best of Breed wins over specials when she was still in the puppy classes. Their top producer Ch. Sercatep's Strut N Proud did well in competition and was also a multiple group placer for several years. He held the record for most black and silver Champions produced. To date he has some forty-four Champions of the colour to his credit.

Keeping their breeding programme to one of quality not quantity, Debbie and Del have never been involved in competing with numbers. A son of Strut N Proud bred by Margo Heiden – Ch. Sycamore's Sojourner – was the next top producer at Sercatep. Amongst his winning progeny were the top-winning pepper and salt bitch Ch. Loneares Leather N Lace, bred by Beth Ann Santire, and their own Ch. Sercateps Nite Flite who became their fourth generation in the top producer listings.

Needing some new blood, the Herrells were able to purchase from the Garmakers a puppy bitch, sired by the outstanding producer Ch. Rampages Waco Kid, from the show ring at

Am. Ch. Sercatep's Nite Flite.

Am. Ch. Sercatep's Jer Red Cedar.

Montgomery County, by name Ch. Repetitions Twist of Fate. She was finished with five majors by the Garmakers. She combined with Strut N Proud lines and gave two outstanding black and silvers – Ch. Sercatep's Strut N Stuff and Ch. Sercatep's Jer Red Cedar – the latter being the number one black and silver for 1990.

For the next five years the Herrells did little breeding and showing of their own dogs but concentrated on their commitments to show for other breeders. Ch. Sercateps Truth or Dare was presented with an Award of Merit under Judge Jon Cole at the 1995 Montgomery County Show – the first black and silver to accomplish this. He has a Specialty best and just missed being the top black and silver that year by just a few points. The following year, although not seriously campaigned until May, he was the year's top black and silver all systems breeder/owner handled. At the same time in Sweden, Ewa-Marie and Leif Nack Holm's black and silver Ch. Sercatep's Falkendal's Aces High was competing successfully to be the top Miniature in Sweden. Truth or Dare's sire is a full brother to Aces High. Debbie and Del Herrell are justifiably proud of both these achievements. With their exports the Sercatep's have also given a sound base for the Miniatures in Scandinavia, particularly the black and silvers.

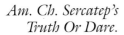

Am. Ch. Sercatep's Truth Or Dare.

11 THE MINIATURE SCHNAUZER IN SCANDINAVIA

The Miniature Schnauzer, in all colours, is gaining more and more supporters in the Scandinavian countries, both as a family dog and at shows, where these dogs are beginning to enjoy some good wins against the other breeds at the national and international shows. With this growing interest, and as imports exert their influence, inevitably differences of opinion surface between those who support the German ideal and those who prefer the American type. Whites, too, are also being bred, which is another area of differing opinion. The Scandinavian shows all come under the FCI umbrella and Breed Standards and, although there is only one parent club – The Pinscher Schnauzer Club – several Pinscher-Schnauzer breed shows are held during the year.

BLACK AND SILVER

SWEDEN
In Sweden the very first black and silver was registered in 1982 from pepper and salt parents, and the first Champion in

the colour was Ch. Jobabs Dilemma, who finished in 1983. His name implies exactly what he was at that time – a dilemma. After he paved the way, other breeders began to import more dogs, at first mainly from Germany, and then from America, Britain and Italy. One of the earliest German imports was Int. Swedish Ch. Lütz vd Steinhäger Heide who sired many Champions and who is still at stud. He is owned by Agneta Rådberg (Mascars) who also breeds pepper and salt Standards.

Anne Wallin (Fixus) imported several dogs from England, including Sw. Ch. Sybray Fixus A Silver Boy (Proscenium Bilbo Baggins ex Ripplevale Frosty Kiss N Hug), who proved to be a popular stud and who sired several Champions. Nina Karlsdotter (Impacts) was also working with English bloodlines, but she has imported several blacks from America that carried the black and silver gene.

Pamela Morrison-Bell also sent semen from Sea-Conflict of Eastwight, a Rownhams Impresario son, to Corinne and Bo Skalin (Hassan-Hills) and the

American-bred Swedish & Danish Ch. Sercatep Falkendal Aces High (Am. Ch. Loneacre's Patton Leather ex Sercatep's Twist N Shout).
Bred by Debbie Herrell (USA), owned by Eva-Marie Nackholm (Sweden).
Top-winning Miniature (all colours) in Sweden 1995 and 1996.

Italian, Swedish & Int. Ch. Scedir Uncas (Int. Ch. Scedir Charlie Brown ex Int. Ch. Scedir Armony). Bred by Fabio Ferrari in Italy, owned by Britt-Marie Israelsson (Bribories kennel) in Sweden. Imported at the age of two, this dog is a Best in Show winner and holds the most titles for a Miniature in Sweden (all colours).

first artificial insemination was carried out. A male from this litter, Sw. Ch. Hassan Hills Dudley, proved to be an influential stud.

The big breakthrough for the black and silver colour in Sweden came when breeders started to import dogs from America. In the beginning it was sometimes difficult to get the judges to accept the softer furnishings and different way of grooming. The imports also had other qualities that the breed badly needed, such as more neck, better toplines and better movement – and, most of all, temperament was greatly improved through the American breeding.

June Hällblad and Sennart Bergqvist

(Kennel Backstreet) imported several dogs from Marcia Feld (Feldmar). They were the first to get the American type accepted by the judges and they have done a lot for the black and silver colour in Sweden. Their Sw. Ch. Feldmar Son Of A Gun, a son of Am. Ch. Feldmar Pistol Pete, was the top winning black and silver from 1992 to 1994, with two Group wins and other placements in that time.

Eve-Marie and Leif Näckholm (Falkendal's) imported dogs from Debbie Herrell (Sercatep) in America,

Italian-bred Swedish Ch. Scedir Flamenco (American-bred Int. Ch. Feldmars Scedir Midnite Dream ex Scedir Quindi).
Bred by Fabio Ferrari (Italy), owned by Eva-Marie Nackholm (Falkendal's kennel) in Sweden.
Not extensively shown but a Best in Show & Group winner.

and the multi-titled Sercatep Falkendal Aces High was the leading Schnauzer of all colours and all sizes for 1995 and 1996. To date his most prestigious win was Group One and Reserve Best in Show at Gothenberg 1995, the same year that he qualified for the coveted invitational Champion of Champions contest. He also had a Group One win and four Best in Show in Denmark in 1996. To date he has around thirty-five Best of Breed and twenty Group placements.

With the change in the quarantine regulations, which now require rabies tests instead of quarantine, breeders have started to import more dogs and bitches from Europe, as well as being able to cross the various Scandinavian borders to show and to breed. One of the dogs that has the most titles in Sweden is the multi-titled and multi-winner Scedir Uncas. He was already two years old and Italian Champion and a big winner when he was imported from Italy. He joined Britt-Marie Israelsson (Bribories) who added further titles to his impressive list. She also owns the outstanding black and silver bitch, Sw. Ch. Sercatep Bribories Nite Kiss, a grand-daughter of Am. Ch. Rampages Representative, and is yet another excellent Miniature exported by Debbie Herrell.

NORWAY AND DENMARK

The black and silver has not become so popular in Norway as elsewhere and, to date, they do not have the quality that is in the other Scandinavian countries, although now, in the late nineties, they are beginning to improve in both numbers and quality, particularly through their Swedish imports. Aud Hermansen (L'est Jardin's) is a breeder who is playing a prominent part in this improvement and is mixing the Feldmar and Sercatep lines with very good results.

In Denmark the influence has been more German than in any other Scandinavian country – that is in both bloodlines *and* grooming. Some breeders do appreciate the American lines, but even so, it is still an uphill struggle to show dogs with furnishings unless the judge is Swedish, British, or American, or a lover of the American style. In Norway some breeders are working with similar lines to those in Sweden and Finland but, at the present time, it is the German lines that predominate. The Italian-bred Ch. Scedir Shirley Tempol, owned by Annelise Lange (Nero Argento), was the leading black and silver in 1996 and the number two Miniature overall.

Italian-bred Danish & Swedish Ch. Scedir Shirley Tempol (Italian Ch. Falkendal's King of Diamond ex Scedir Ladyginevra). Bred by Fabio Ferrari in Italy, owned by Annelise Lange (Nero Argento kennels) in Denmark. Top-winning black & silver in Denmark 1996 and a Best in Show winner.

FINLAND

The Italian Scedir lines of Fabio Ferrari have dominated the black and silver breeding in Finland. One of the first to start with the colour was Soile Bister (Trixer), who imported the bitch Ch. Schnauzi's Melissa from Frieda Steiger of Switzerland, using exactly the same bloodlines as Fabio Ferrari had first started with in Italy. Melissa's sire, Schnauzi's Pyewacket, was sired by Frieda Steiger's Canadian black and silver import, Tribute's Tuxedo Junction, who proved to be the cornerstone for black and silver breeding in Europe. Before she went to Finland, Melissa had a litter by the Israeli-bred Chatifa Bar Lutz, which contained Schnauzi's Black Jack who, as has been mentioned earlier, joined Fabio Ferrari in Italy.

PEPPER AND SALT

SWEDEN

Pauline Bjoerklund, with the Motown Miniatures, is a prominent breeder and exhibitor, and her dogs have done considerable winning in the breed in recent years. Her home-bred bitch, the multi-titled Ch. Motowns Rock Olga, is the most winning pepper and salt at the present time. She was the Pinscher-Schnauzer Club's Dog of the Year in 1995, as well as enjoying a Best Puppy in Show and three times Best in Show at the major breed events. Her sire is the top stud Int. Ch. Brittovans Mac The Knife Motown. With her early breeding based on Deansgate imports, Ms. Bjoerklund nowadays concentrates on an input of Ch. Travelmors US Mail blood into her line.

The talented ceramic sculptress Gunilla Agronius, with the Prefix Miniatures, is another who has bred and shown good pepper and salts, but she now concentrates on her Chinese Cresteds. Her veteran male, Int. Ch. Prefix Jultomte, is a third-generation of home-bred international title holders and a producing stud for Scandinavia, with several Champions to his credit. His half-sister, Prefix Dolly Parton, is a good producer and is now a veteran. She qualified for the Swedish Veteran of Veterans sponsored competition.

Ewa-Marie and Leif Näckholm are branching out into pepper and salts to run in tandem with their most successful black and silver Miniatures. Debbra Herrell (Sercateps) has provided their foundation for this line, just as she did for their black and silvers. She has sent over the American-bred male, Sercateps Secret Agent. He is already a Swedish and Danish Champion, on only limited showing. For their foundation bitches they have imported, from Risepark, the Ch. Repetitions Favorite Son For Risepark daughter, Risepark Favorite Girl, who is already a multi-titled winner, and the Ch. Malenda Masterblend at Risepark daughter, Risepark Falkendal Queen, who is already a National Champion and Best in Show winner.

NORWAY AND FINLAND

In Norway two male imports, both by Ch. Trevelmors US Mail, have had the biggest influence on breeding and showing today. They are UK and Int. Ch. Ashwick Mr. Pickwick, bred and exported by Pam and Dave Wick and owned by Anders Hanssen, and Geir Kvael's Int. Ch. Malenda Morning Mail,

*Swedish, Finnish Ch. Nordic'97
Winner Risepark Favorite Girl
(American-bred Ch. Repetitions
Favorite Son For Risepark ex
Risepark Dayline Debutante).
Bred by Newman & Day, owned and
exhibited by Eva-Marie Näckholm
(Falkendal's kennel) in Sweden.*

*Swedish & Nordic Ch. Risepark
Falkendal's Queen (Ch. Malenda
Master Blend at Risepark ex Risepark
Blues on Parade).
Bred by Newman & Day, owned by
Eva-Marie Näckholm (Sweden).*

sent out by his breeder, Glenys Allen.
Both are Best in Show and Group
winners and both have Champions to
their credit. In bitches, Wrendras
Christmas Carol was imported by Astrid
and Torbjoern Welle, and Motowns
Zazza Gabor, owned by Hilde
Haakensen, has her national title and was
sent by her breeder, Pauline Bjoerkland.
These, too, have been influential. With
the pepper and salts in Finland, those
with the German look and breeding are,
in the main, those that find favour both
in the show ring and with the breeding.

BLACKS
Geri Kelly's blacks have been sent to all
parts of the world and, in Scandinavia,
the multi-titled Ch. Kelly's Pepalfa's
New Star is one of Sweden's top-
winning Miniatures ever, having been
shown fifty-five times and going Best of
Breed on fifty-one occasions. He was
twice Best in Show at an International
show, he is a multi-Group winner as well
having four Specialty bests and he is also
three-times Pinscher-Schnauzer Club
Dog of the Year. He is owned by Gunilla
and Bengt Nyden.

*Norwegian Ch. Malenda
Martegon (American bred Ch.
Travelmors US Mail ex Ch.
Malenda Moschetel).
Bred in England by Mrs Allen
(photographed at seven months).*